PRESENTED TO:

_____

FROM:

_____

DATE:

_____

INDIVISIBLE

One Marriage Under God

ROBERT NOLAND

THOMAS NELSON
Since 1798

Published in Nashville, Tennessee, by Thomas Nelson. Thomas Nelson is a registered trademark of HarperCollins Christian Publishing, Inc.

Published in association with the literary agency of WTA Services, LLC, Franklin, Tennessee.

Thomas Nelson titles may be purchased in bulk for educational, business, fund-raising, or sales promotional use. For information, please email SpecialMarkets@ThomasNelson.com.

ISBN: 978–1–4002–1100–5

Printed in China

18 19 20 21 22 23 TIMS 6 5 4 3 2 1

CONTENTS

FOREWORD

Heather and I knew beyond a shadow of a doubt that God had called us together for one another, and for His plan and purposes. When I joined the military as a chaplain, it was a mutual decision for us. We knew that God would use us both to minister together as well as separately to reach those who had volunteered to die for us, if called upon.

In May 2007, I was deployed to Iraq with the 1st Battalion, 30th Infantry Regiment for fifteen months during the military surge in Iraq, leaving Heather and our three children at home. That separation alone, aside from the high-risk area where we were assigned, was extremely difficult. Every day we fought an invisible enemy, searching booby-trapped houses, traveling IED-laden roads, and wondering who in our path was friend or foe. But I had no idea that when I would return, I would be carrying a very different, yet just as deadly, invisible enemy with me, one that would place our family in the battle for our lives, not in a foreign country, but inside the four walls of our own home.

After my return to the base in Georgia in the summer of

2008, the overwhelming grief, shock, rage, anxiety, depression, and extreme sadness over what I had experienced on the battle lines—all the same issues for which I had counseled, served, and ministered to the soldiers—overtook and overwhelmed me. I came home physically whole with no visible handicaps or injuries, but my mind and heart were wounded and bleeding profusely from losing men and women with whom I had served and whom I had come to dearly love. But before long, that which was bottled up tight under pressure and shaken began to explode, and I was taking my pain out on Heather and the kids, emotionally and verbally.

Within a few months, one day while grasping at the end of her rope, Heather told me to leave—to get out of the house. The strong and committed Christian couple we had been, called to minister to others in Jesus' name, was now far away, questioning everything. Struggling to survive, I left the army in August of 2009 and went to work at a local Home Depot.

One day, one step, one crawl at a time, through hard work together with our love for God and love for one another, eventually I started to gain ground and find healing, and the process of reconciliation began. Four long months later, we started over, allowing God to do what only He can do in any marriage that will submit to the restoration of oneness He miraculously creates between a man and a woman committed to one another.

Over time, we made the decision together to return to the army chaplaincy, offering God *all* of our experiences—from the mountaintop moments to the valley of the shadow of death—to serve military families once again. Still to this day, as we write this foreword, we are serving our great God and this wonderful country at Fort Bragg, North Carolina.

Regardless of whether you have been in the military, the

daily demands and dilemmas with which we are confronted in this world challenge us all, especially in marriage. Problems stay in our faces, while answers seem elusive. That is today's unmistakable reality. But Heather and I want to drive home, through the film *Indivisible* as well as this devotional book, one clear and essential fact: the only answer for how a marriage can not only survive but thrive and be successful today is Jesus Christ. We have seen that truth proven firsthand in our own lives. That is the reason for our marriage, our ministry, the film, this book, and all that we put our hearts, minds, and hands to for Him.

We pray that in these pages you find help, healing, hope, inspiration, motivation, and a fresh vision for your own marriage to create connection, experience a new place of oneness, and forge a deeper bond as a couple than ever before. But more than anything, Heather and I want you to come to know and follow the Creator and Author of love, Jesus Christ.

CH (MAJ) Darren and Heather Turner

INTRODUCTION

We are so glad that you have chosen to connect your marriage relationship with this devotional, *Indivisible*. The major motion picture of the same name is the true story of army chaplain Darren Turner and his wife, Heather, the authors of the foreword. Four of Darren's and one of Heather's actual journal entries from Darren's fifteen-month deployment in Iraq are included in the book.

Whether you are a military couple or not, are engaged, newly married, looking for a refresh or reset in your relationship, or you have picked up this book out of total desperation for your marriage, these authentic truths, Scripture passages, and practical exercises can encourage you to a new and deeper bond. We pray that in these pages you consistently discover three key elements that God has made available for your marriage: help, healing, and hope.

The Creator of life, love, and the marital union wants to give you these three gifts from His own heart, no matter where you are in your relationship today. With God as the invited Guest into your home over these next fifty days, your *connection* can become more intimate, your *commitment* can become indivisible, and your *community* with others will be invaluable in the kingdom of God as a witness for Christ.

If at all possible, dive in together and engage with each day. If your spouse will not commit to join you, we want to encourage and empower you to dig in and apply the truths you find to your own life and contribution to your marriage. While the days are written for couples to experience together, you can easily translate the text to your personal circumstances and commitment.

Here are a few helps for success as you experience *Indivisible*:

1. *Decide to commit.*

    Purpose to use this book for the next fifty days, setting aside the intentional and undistracted time to make a habit of engaging with the words contained here. If you miss a day or two, just pick back up where you left off. Please don't give in to the temptation to feel any guilt; just get back on board. Don't quit—commit. Your marriage is worth every moment you invest.

2. *Pick a time.*

    Discuss and choose together the optimum time for your schedule. Compromise to work out this important detail. You may need to experiment a bit, but pick a time and stick with it. We will all find the moments for the things that matter most to us.

3. *Choose a place.*

    Pick the most comfortable setting away from distractions. No phones. No devices. No TV and no one else around. The environment is crucial for you both to be focused and comfortable as you engage with one another and with God.

4. *Read.*

Take in all the content. Don't scan, as you would a text or email, but carefully read it like a love letter, most especially the Bible verses. If you prefer to use your own version of Scripture each day, feel free to do so. Just look up the verses and read your Bible instead.

5. *Create connection.*

The final section of each of the fifty days is a practical application step for you to take. The goal is to create intentional and intimate connection between the two of you and God. There are clear instructions for each activity. These are simple, realistic ways your marriage can grow in depth and maturity. Many days facilitate discussion as an intentional exercise to improve and deepen your communication. Following the exercise are three questions to help you think through, evaluate, and process the outcome. If you find it is optimal for you to begin each day with the questions from the previous day, feel free to do so. This section is likely the most important part of each day with the opportunity to turn knowledge into application, and then into real and lasting change. When you complete the fifty days and have done each of these "Creating Connection" activities, you will likely both *see* and *experience* your marital and spiritual growth.

6. *Pray.*

If you have never spent time in consistent prayer together as a couple, the next fifty days could revolutionize your marriage. Allow a few moments at the end of every day to speak with God together, telling Him everything as you would a best friend. Just talk to Him.

Be honest. Be specific. No fancy, spiritual language is necessary. Tell Him what's on each of your hearts.

7. *Follow through.*

The goal of these fifty days is to allow Jesus Christ to change your marriage and your lives. Following the completion of this book, from your fifty-first day onward, success will come as together you listen to the voice of God and walk with Him.

"What you say to one another is eternal. I mean this. When two of you get together on anything at all on earth and make a prayer of it, my Father in heaven goes into action. And when two or three of you are together because of me, you can be sure that I'll be there."

Matthew 18:20 MSG

DAY 1

IMPOSSIBLE POSSIBILITIES

Jesus looked at them and said, "With man this is impossible,
but not with God; all things are possible with God."

Mark 10:27

Do you ever look at a couple with deep admiration because their marriage just seems to exist for a greater purpose? You see the husband and wife thrive together, and their relationship is a thing of beauty, not only for each other, but also as an example for other couples to follow. The great news is that any marriage, over time, can arrive at such a place—even yours.

The one word that needs to come alive in your marriage as you engage the pages of this book is *hope*. Hope can offer a fresh start and bring a new vision. Hope can lead you to say, "We can," instead of, "We can't." Hope can help you say, "We will," rather than, "We won't."

But how can your perspective change? How can you enter a new season in which you choose hope and believe the best for you and your mate? There is only one way, just one road to real and authentic hope: Jesus.

Jesus had just encountered a wealthy, young man who had asked Him how he could have eternal life. Christ, knowing the man's circumstances, could see that he was fully dependent on his bank account and his own ability to be "good." He'd even told Jesus that he had obeyed all the commandments since he was young, which, of course, was impossible. Jesus told him that there was one thing he lacked: "Go, sell everything you have and give to the poor, and you will have treasure in heaven. Then come, follow me" (Mark 10:21).

The young man responded to Jesus by silently walking away. When those who had witnessed this exchange began to wonder how *anyone* could get into God's kingdom, Jesus answered with today's verse: "With man this is impossible, but not with God."

We, too, can tend to rely on our resources and our own abilities to live life, just as the wealthy man in this story was doing. But we can also be our own hindrance to discovering real life and authentic hope. As with a trust fall, sometimes we have to let go of the familiar to experience faith.

Have you come to believe there are some things in your marriage that are "impossible"? Are there places you want to go in your relationship but just can't see how? Regardless of your answers, your new truth can be: *But not with God: all things are possible with God.* The answer for your marriage is the same as it was for the man in this story: *follow Jesus.* After all, what have you got to lose? Or more accurately, if "all things are possible with God"—what do you have to *gain*?

Creating Connection

It's time to dream big together for your marriage. Discuss the qualities in couples that you admire. Write down every descriptive word for the kind of marriage you would like to have. Think big and be generous. Don't hold back what you want to see and experience for one another and your relationship. After you complete your list of goals and dreams, pray a simple prayer, asking God to help you both seek together what is possible through Him. Consider placing today's verse somewhere you both can see it daily as a reminder of your Source of hope.

1. How did it feel to dream and express hope for your marriage?

_____

_____

_____

_____

_____

_____

_____

_____

2. Were you both in agreement on the list of goals and desires?

_____

_____

_____

_____

_____

_____

3. How can the introduction of hope and the letting go of your own abilities and shortcomings help you reach your dreams for your marriage?

_____

_____

_____

_____

_____

_____

IMPOSSIBILITIES BECOME POSSIBLE WITH GOD.

DAY 2

THE LEGACY OF LOVE

He died for all, that those who live should no longer live
for themselves but for him who died for them and was
raised again. So from now on we regard no one from a
worldly point of view. Though we once regarded Christ
in this way, we do so no longer. Therefore, if anyone is
in Christ, the new creation has come: The old has gone,
the new is here! All this is from God, who reconciled us
to himself through Christ.

2 Corinthians 5:15–18

The film *Indivisible*, depicting the true story of Darren and
Heather Turner, is one of tragedy and triumph, life and
death, gut-wrenching grief, and amazing grace. Throughout
their story, we see that the foundation of their lives and marriage is a personal relationship with Jesus Christ. Decisions they
made together as a couple, callings they both followed, and the
strength on which they leaned during the most difficult of days
all came from a deep faith in a personal God.

Regardless of why you are reading this devotional, your past or present circumstances, how healthy or horrible your marriage may be, it is vital as you move forward in these pages to understand the simple gospel, found in today's scripture, that the Turners believe saved their lives as well as their marriage.

Because of God's great love for His creation, He made the choice to allow free will from the very beginning. Adam and Eve were not programmed robots that could only choose their Creator, but rather they were given the choice to follow Him or their own ways. In the moment of truth in the garden, when confronted by God's enemy, they chose to disobey the one rule given amid all their freedom, and then sin entered humankind's DNA forever.

The reason the gospel is called the good news is found in our Bible passage today. Christ, the only Son of God, made His own choice to enter earth and make it clear throughout history who He was and that His mission was to seek and to save that which had been lost (Luke 19:10). He went to the cross, sacrificing His own life for our choices, conquered death and the grave, and rose again to new life. This act of love built a bridge, giving each of us the opportunity to choose Him. But God leaves this individual decision up to us.

The Bible states that in Christ we become a "new creation." That means our spirits reconnect to the original state in the garden, and we can have a personal relationship with God as Adam and Eve first had. This is what Christ provided and now offers to everyone.

If, in your marriage, you never or rarely have spiritual conversations, or maybe such talks have even been difficult in the past, try this: regardless of your past history or beliefs, agree to wipe the slate clean for a few minutes and read today's Bible passage together, as well as the paragraphs that give explanation of the gospel. Focus on the simple truth of what Christ has done and now offers you. Could this possibly be a choice for you to make together for a fresh start, not only in your marriage but also in your individual lives? What God did for Darren and Heather Turner is not at all exclusive but is available to any and every couple. That is the beauty of the good news!

1. What did today's Bible passage reveal to you?

_____

_____

_____

_____

_____

_____

_____

_____

2. Do you feel that exploring spiritual discussions together can help you? Why or why not?

_____

_____

_____

_____

_____

3. If either or both of you made a spiritual decision for a fresh start, share the experience together and write down what happened. If so, this day marks a turning point in your life and relationship.

_____

_____

_____

_____

_____

CHRIST WANTS TO MAKE YOUR HOME, HIS HOME.

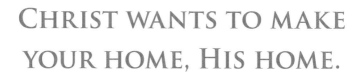

DAY 3

BECOMING ONE

"Haven't you read," he replied, "that at the beginning
the Creator 'made them male and female,' and said, 'For
this reason a man will leave his father and mother and be
united to his wife, and the two will become one flesh'?
So they are no longer two, but one flesh. Therefore what
God has joined together, let no one separate."

Matthew 19:4–6

The word *indivisible* is most often associated in our culture
with the United States' Pledge of Allegiance, reinforcing the
idea of a nation unable to be separated into parts and divided.
But simply vowing to live indivisibly does not mean harmful
external and internal forces will not engage and encroach. We
live in a day when our unity is constantly challenged and division seems to be the more common outcome.

Similarly, even in society's foundational relationship of marriage, the God-ordained institution created for and between a
man and woman is regularly tested in these volatile times.

But even the most common marriage vows recited today still reflect this idea of an unshakable bond being created: "I take you to be my lawfully wedded husband/wife, to have and to hold, from this day forward, for better, for worse, for richer, for poorer, in sickness and health, until death do us part."

The nation's forefathers did not create this concept of indivisibility, but rather God Himself, for His divine purpose of marriage. Jesus connected the idea of a marital union being indivisible through His teaching. One day some of the Pharisees were conducting their regular testing of Christ and decided to bring up marriage. Today's scripture contains His response as He referenced God's words in Genesis 1 and 2. Notice especially where He says the husband and wife are "joined together."

To offer a simple analogy of being indivisible or "joined together," imagine tearing off two equal-size pieces from a roll of duct tape. Separate, the two sections are very sticky. In fact, you have to be careful that they don't bond to something prematurely before you apply them to their intended target. If you carefully connect their sticky sides, matching up corner to corner, pressing together all the way around both, you will effectively no longer have two pieces of tape, but one single unit. They have fully bonded to one another. If you try to separate them, you cannot successfully divide the two, but only destroy both, for they are now truly indivisible.

Creating Connection

Using Christ's "one flesh" concept, coupled with today's analogy, tear off two equal-size pieces of duct tape, keeping them separated. (If you want to get really creative, go to a craft store and get a roll of each of your favorite colors or styles.) With each of you holding your piece of duct tape, carefully line them up and press them together to form one indivisible unit. Keep the bonded tape in a special place that each of you can see to constantly remind you of your "indivisibility."

1. How did you each respond to the "duct tape ceremony"?

_____

_____

_____

_____

_____

_____

_____

_____

_____

_____

2. Did this give you any insights or thoughts about the bond of your relationship?

_____

_____

_____

_____

_____

3. Did you decide to display the tape in a place to remind you both of your unity?

_____

_____

_____

_____

_____

INDIVISIBLE MARRIAGES ARE BONDED TOGETHER FOR LIFE.

GATHERING YOUR GET-TO'S

Because of our faith, Christ has brought us into this place of undeserved privilege where we now stand, and we confidently and joyfully look forward to sharing God's glory. We can rejoice, too, when we run into problems and trials, for we know that they help us develop endurance.

Romans 5:2–3 NLT

"I *get to* go on vacation next week." "I *have to* attend a training seminar tomorrow." "We *get to* go to dinner with the Smiths tonight." "We *have to* go to the Johnsons' this weekend." There are some things in life that will always be "get-to's" while others remain "have-to's." Sometimes the difference between the two is a very real obstacle, while in other circumstances it simply requires a perspective change.

One of the great ironies of the human existence is that things in our lives that start out as "get-to's" can become "have-to's." In marriage, as the years go by and responsibilities mount, it is often easy to allow the privileges we were once so excited to experience together to slowly convert into daily problems we must continually try to solve.

God made His salvation a "get-to," not a "have-to." He forces no one into trusting Him. It's a very personal choice that no one can make but you. But once you accept His gracious offer of redemption, all of life can become a privilege and can be seen through His perspective. Even your problems can turn into opportunities, as verse 3 shows.

One of the great "get-to's" of life is marriage. Our self-ishness and sin are what turns this divine gift into anything else. The wonderful hope and encouragement we have through Christ in all our relationships, but most especially in marriage, is that He can turn our perspective of any "have-to" into a "get-to" as we "confidently and joyfully look forward to sharing God's glory."

Filtering your marriage through today's Bible passage, your relationship is most certainly an "undeserved privilege" in which you and your spouse have the amazing opportunity to join together in a relationship with God. That is part of what a Christian marriage is all about—serving Him together. In fact, any of the "problems and trials" you are experiencing right now are things He can and wants to use to help you both "develop endurance" as you grow and mature together in Him.

Creating Connection

You likely know many of each other's "have-to's" and "get-to's." Think through those carefully for a moment, and write down any that come to mind. Each of you choose one "have-to" from the other's list that you know you could take over from your spouse for the day. Next, choose one "get-to" that you can provide for the other. As soon as possible for your mate, make these happen. They don't have to be elaborate or expensive; focus on simply being thoughtful and kind. Replenishing your spouse through helpful acts of service is a great connector.

1. How did these gifts of service to one another make you feel?

_____

_____

_____

_____

_____

_____

_____

_____

2. How does seeing your mate's response to a kindness motivate you?

_____

_____

_____

_____

_____

3. How can you create more of these replenishing moments in your marriage, knocking out some "have-to's" and adding on some "get-to's" for one another?

_____

_____

_____

_____

_____

LIFE WILL ALWAYS BRING PLENTY OF "HAVE-TO'S," SO COMMIT TO CREATING "GET-TO'S" IN YOUR MARRIAGE.

DAY 5

INTENTIONAL TIMES

While they were eating, Jesus took bread, and when he had given thanks, he broke it and gave it to his disciples, saying, "Take and eat; this is my body." Then he took a cup, and when he had given thanks, he gave it to them, saying, "Drink from it, all of you. This is my blood of the covenant, which is poured out for many for the forgiveness of sins. I tell you, I will not drink from this fruit of the vine from now on until that day when I drink it new with you in my Father's kingdom."

Matthew 26:26–29

From Chaplain Darren Turner's journal:

I am home (Canton, GA) on leave. This leave is especially important because it is my final time off before I deploy to Iraq for 15 months. Having a going-away party this weekend is a very strange feeling. Sad but anxious to go, all at the same time; so hard to explain. God willing, I will return to them healthy and unharmed. But there's always the possibility that something bad will happen. Everyone around me knows and feels this. I can sense it with everyone. It's never said but it's there. I know. And I know they know.

I'm glad they're concerned because some soldiers, God bless them, don't have any family, much less family committed enough to throw a party. I am blessed. I am thankful. I just pray that everything that needs to be said this weekend will be said.

The last-time-I-will-do-this mentality is alive and well. I'm having lots of "last times" with family members before I leave. Being intentional is suddenly more important than it used to be. I'd like to think I could keep it this way.

Jesus also knew the uncertainty and pain of "the-last-time-I-will-do-this" moments. He experienced those with His disciples before going to the cross. One of those best-known "last times" was the Last Supper. In obedience to His example, we relive that moment regularly in our churches today to remember Christ's sacrifice for us.

A sad but all-too-frequent regret heard from a surviving spouse following a death in a marriage is, "If only I had been able to say goodbye" or "If I had known that was going to be the last time I would see him/her, I would have made certain I expressed my love."

In your own marriage, imagine if this week were filled with "last times" between you and your spouse, whether for the next fifteen months or even forever. How would such thoughts change your attitude? Would you approach normal, day-to-day moments differently? If so, how?

Creating Connection

With this same mind-set, plan a special date. Whether it be a quiet evening alone with the phones put away to just share and catch up, a night out for dinner and some fun, or even having personal Communion with just the two of you, create a special moment to remember. Be sure to express anything you would want to say to each other if it were the last time you would see one another. To echo Darren's words, be sure everything that needs to be said is said. Be intentional.

1. Was there anything that felt different about this special time together?

_____

_____

_____

_____

_____

_____

_____

_____

_____

_____

2. How did you approach this date differently, and why?

_____

_____

_____

_____

_____

_____

3. What was the best thing about this intentional time together?

_____

_____

_____

_____

_____

_____

"LAST TIME" THOUGHTS CAN BRING BACK "FIRST TIME" FEELINGS.

BUILDING ON BEDROCK

"Everyone who hears these words of mine and puts them into practice is like a wise man who built his house on the rock. The rain came down, the streams rose, and the winds blew and beat against that house; yet it did not fall, because it had its foundation on the rock. But everyone who hears these words of mine and does not put them into practice is like a foolish man who built his house on sand. The rain came down, the streams rose, and the winds blew and beat against that house, and it fell with a great crash."

Matthew 7:24–27

A congregation was constructing a new church building at another location in the city. The pastor decided to go out and visit the jobsite for the first time. As he put on his hard hat and walked up to the emerging structure, he saw three bricklayers working alone on three different walls.

The pastor went to the first bricklayer and asked, "What

are you doing there, sir?" The man snarled and sarcastically answered, "I'm setting this brick on this wall." The pastor then went to the second man and asked, "What are you doing there, sir?" He looked at the minister, back at the structure, and then stated, "I'm building a wall." The pastor then walked to the third and final man and asked, "What are you doing there, sir?" The bricklayer stepped back, flashed a big grin at the pastor, and shouted, "I'm building a church!"

You could walk up to three different husbands or wives today to ask each one about his or her marriage and quite possibly get answers very similar to the bricklayers'. Some will just be coexisting, trying to merely get through another day. Others seem happy and satisfied at simply doing life together. But then there will be a precious few who realize they are building something beautiful, extraordinary, and spiritual as a couple. Something they could never create alone. And something they could never construct without God being right in the midst of their relationship.

Building a relational foundation on sinking sand, as in today's scripture, is actually very easy to do. But that is exactly why, when the storms of life threaten, so many marital "houses" crash down around the couple. That's the bad news. The great news is, the stability and firm foundation of Christ are offered to any couple who will surrender their lives to Him. Those marriages that choose together to build on and make Him their Rock have a far greater opportunity to keep their "house" safe and secure in the storms. Not that these couples won't have challenges or problems—they most certainly will, as all marriages do—but they have simply decided together on whom they will depend, no matter the circumstances.

While lengthy physical distance, as Darren and Heather Turner had to endure while he was deployed to Iraq, will always be difficult and demanding, emotional distance while living in the same house is one of the deadliest poisons in marriages. Today, seek to create an *emotional*, nonsexual connection with each other through an intentional expression of love, such as a long embrace just because, a note expressing how you feel, or even a greeting card mailed from work to your spouse at home or to your spouse's workplace. Find a unique and personalized way to draw each other's hearts together in authentic closeness and affection. This is a keystone in the foundation on which your marriage is built.

1. How did this connection impact your marriage emotionally?

_____

_____

_____

_____

_____

_____

2. Following this expression of love and affection, did you sense a decrease in any distance gap that was present before?

_____

_____

_____

_____

_____

3. How can you place a more intentional focus on the emotional side of your marriage?

_____

_____

_____

_____

_____

ANY ACT OF OBEDIENCE TO CHRIST IN YOUR MARRIAGE EXPANDS AND DEEPENS THE FOUNDATION OF FAITH IT IS BUILT UPON.

DAY 7

TALKING POINTS

My dear brothers and sisters, take note of this: Everyone should be quick to listen, slow to speak and slow to become angry.

James 1:19

At lunch with one of her friends, a young lady who was a newlywed was overheard answering a question about her and her husband's emerging communication style in their marriage. She shared, "Well, we have a great relationship so far. He graduated from college as a communications major, and I received my degree in theater. So he is very articulate when he speaks, and I act like I'm listening."

For many years, real estate agents have said that their top three rules for buying and selling property are "location, location, location." The obvious point of emphasis is the site of the property being the single-most contributing factor to the value.

In this same light, asking marriage counselors about the top three rules for strong and healthy relationships, their answer would likely be "communication, communication, communication." This is why you will never hear anyone in a marriage say, "Our problem is we just communicate way too much."

We live in a culture where vocal domination has become a strategic focus. Whether face-to-face or through social media, voicing what we think has become like a new contact sport. As a result, listening seems to be a dying art form.

How many marital issues would be solved if we heeded James's words: "Be quick to listen, slow to speak"? In our marriages, we do not necessarily need to *hear* more, but certainly we must *listen* more. Active listening to both the words and the nonverbal cues our spouses communicate through the face and body is a skill we must constantly hone. We will never arrive, so this will take an ongoing commitment of focus and energy.

On the other side of communication, we must also make our words count. The wise are not silent but are proactively listening, with the ongoing goal of saying the right thing at the right time in the right way.

Each of you think for a moment about where you are too quick to speak. Where are you slow to listen, or maybe have stopped listening at all, like the young newlywed in today's story? Is there any area where you can specifically line up your actions with today's verse? Communication will always be a challenge, even in the best of marriages, but it can also be an incredible blessing as you grow closer together in both your verbal and nonverbal contact.

Creating Connection

Today, each of you make a personal commitment with your mouth to be "slow to speak" and with your ears to be "quick to listen" in communicating with each other. Choose to speak only positive and uplifting words for the next twenty-four hours, regardless of what the other may say or not say. Don't try to accomplish this by avoiding communication or conflict, but proactively speak, call, or text only intentionally encouraging words. Ask God to make your every word spoken into a blessing for one another.

1. How did you each respond to this day of positive communication?

_____

_____

_____

_____

_____

_____

_____

_____

_____

_____

2. How did this decision affect your words? Were there times you chose not to speak?

_____

_____

_____

_____

_____

_____

3. What is one positive thing that occurred in your marriage because of your efforts?

_____

_____

_____

_____

_____

_____

LET YOUR WORDS BUILD BRIDGES AND BREAK DOWN BARRIERS IN YOUR MARRIAGE.

ONE + ONE = ONE

"Because of this, a man leaves father and mother, and in marriage he becomes one flesh with a woman—no longer two individuals, but forming a new unity. Because God created this organic union of the two sexes, no one should desecrate his art by cutting them apart."

Mark 10:7-9 MSG

A pastor and his wife were known by the people in their church to have a strong marriage and often did marital counseling together with couples in the church and community. They soon began to notice that when people would refer to them, they would say their names by running them together—as if they were one word. His name was Ronald and her name was Rachel, so the new name for the couple, pronounced together, sounded like this: Ronald-'n'-Rachel. To the people who knew them well, the connected names became a single, five-syllable word.

This practice became so noticeable that the couple would

just smile at each other every time they heard their names spoken as one because that was exactly their heart and goal for their marriage as well as their desire for their witness to others.

When a couple gets married, a new entity is created with a new identity. Certainly, the two are still independent and operate as individuals; yet a corporate combination also becomes visible and present to all who know them. For the pastor and his wife, if you just had Ronald or Rachel, that was great; but a new purpose and expectation came when Ronald-'n'-Rachel were together and ministering as one. A *synergy*—the sum being much greater than the individual parts—makes for an experience larger and stronger when combined. In today's verses, note the use of the phrases "forming a new unity," "organic union," and "his art," promoting the concept of synergy that God creates in marriage.

Such is the biblical concept of marriage—what God does in the hearts, souls, lives, and gifts of any couple who calls Him Lord. He creates a visible oneness that doesn't exist in the same manner outside of the two working together. It is indeed a spiritual and mystical mystery that only He can create.

Say your names together quickly with the *'n'* between them. Do you hear and sense the unity created? Do you recognize the life that your marriage gives by the fusion of you both bringing glory to the Lord together? As biblical marriage comes under attack more and more, it becomes critical for Christ followers to commit to placing our focus on creating oneness that can only be explained by the presence and power of almighty God.

Creating Connection

Today, find a creative way to display your names together with the 'n' between them. You could do the old-school activity of carving your names into a tree in the yard. Print and cut out your connected names in a cool font and tape it to the fridge, or write them with a dry-erase marker on the bathroom mirror. Get creative to express your "organic union" in God's "art." Talk about the synergy you create and the witness for Christ you can bring through your persona as a couple.

1. Have you ever noticed the people in your life connecting you and your spouse's names in a run-on style?

_____

_____

_____

_____

_____

_____

_____

_____

_____

2. Do you and your spouse feel that the people in your circles of influence see you as a synergic marriage? Why or why not?

_____

_____

_____

_____

_____

_____

3. What efforts can you make in your relationship to increase your witness as a couple for Christ?

_____

_____

_____

_____

_____

_____

YOUR INDIVIDUAL ENERGY CAN TOGETHER CREATE INCREDIBLE SYNERGY.

DAY 9

CALLED TO THE DANCE

There is a time for everything, and a season for every
activity under the heavens: a time to be born and a time
to die, a time to plant and a time to uproot, a time to
kill and a time to heal, a time to tear down and a time
to build, a time to weep and a time to laugh, a time to
mourn and a time to dance.

Ecclesiastes 3:1-4

Imagine a large, freshly polished ballroom dance floor. The
house lights dim as the spotlight focuses your attention
on a couple strolling out to the center. The man is dressed
in a full tuxedo, and the woman is adorned in a beautiful,
flowing, floor-length ball gown. Individually, they look
amazing. But then they clasp hands, embrace, and as the
music begins, they start to show the world the purpose for
their presence—to display how no one can dance together
quite the way they can.

As one, they move about the floor with style and grace,

33

giving the appearance of effortlessly floating. As the couple syncs perfectly with the music, they are having fun, proud of what they have accomplished and what they are now experiencing together. What is on display is simply beautiful to watch and enjoy. Such is the goal of God in your marriage, for your best and for His glory.

In today's scripture, King Solomon paints a clear picture of the extremes in this life. For humankind throughout history, there are definite seasons, births and deaths, ebbs and flows, victories and failures, sowing and reaping.

In our busy, day-to-day lives, with all the stresses we face, it is so easy to ignore or forget that we are to constantly allow new birth in our lives, harvest the good things of God, heal from our hurts, build up from our failures, and yes, even allow the time to laugh and dance together. God does not want this life to rob us of those pleasures He intends as we work and play together as couples to bring a healthy balance to our lives year in and year out.

Creating Connection

So many weddings, no matter the country of origin, involve the bride and groom dancing together
as a first-time moment in marriage. Most often, the
celebration following the ceremony finds the newlywed couple taking the floor while everyone stops to
witness the festive experience. Such an event in any
wedding is one of joy and laughter for everyone in
attendance. When was the last time the two of you
actually danced together? Tonight, turn the lights
down, put on "your song," embrace, and slow dance,
with no one watching except the One who brought
you together. (If you don't yet have an "our song,"
this is the perfect opportunity to discover one.)

1. Was dancing together easy or awkward? Why?

_____

_____

_____

_____

_____

_____

_____

2. Is it a struggle to allow yourselves the permission to just have some romantic fun?

_____

_____

_____

_____

_____

3. How can you create regular opportunities to laugh and have fun together?

_____

_____

_____

_____

_____

No matter the difficulty of the day, don't forget you have been called to dance together.

DAY 10

A LOVE TO DIE FOR

Dear brothers and sisters, I plead with you to give your bodies to God because of all he has done for you. Let them be a living and holy sacrifice—the kind he will find acceptable. This is truly the way to worship him. Don't copy the behavior and customs of this world, but let God transform you into a new person by changing the way you think. Then you will learn to know God's will for you, which is good and pleasing and perfect.

Romans 12:1–2 NLT

Day to day in marriage, there are the simple requests, such as, "Can you pause your TV show for a few minutes and help me with something?" Then there are the hassled but harmless asks, like, "I know you're really busy, but could you possibly leave early today to pick up the kids?" And finally, there are the potential game changers: "Some things are really bothering me about our relationship, and I think we need to talk tonight."

Marriage constantly requires and challenges us to place our

spouses before our own needs. But this is exactly God's plan to change us into His image—His personal holiness prioritized over our passing happiness. After all, what could be better for a self-centered sinner than to continually place someone else first in the name of love?

Today's scripture talks about "a living and holy sacrifice." A "living sacrifice" is an oxymoron, meaning two words that seem mismatched together. If a sacrifice is laid on the altar to die in the place of someone else, then how can it possibly continue to live? Paul was talking about a state in which we live on the altar of Christ, giving up our "rights" to Him and serving His purposes instead of our own.

As humans, constantly sacrificing for someone else will eventually burn us out and we will fail, always in time defaulting back to our own desires. But as Christ-followers, submitting our will to God keeps us motivated and moving toward the service of others for His sake. That is a totally different perspective and one that is necessary for a growing and healthy marriage.

Think for a moment about the strongest marriages you know in your circles. Consider the marriages that you would most want to imitate. There is a strong chance that those couples also commit to being living sacrifices to the Lord, as well as continually dying to self with one another.

A great evaluation would be to filter your relationship through today's scripture to ask: *Are there any areas of our marriage in which we "copy the behavior and customs of this world"?* And then the follow-up question: *What area of our marriage has been the most transformed by the Lord?*

Creating Connection

Today, simply affirm one another. Speak not only compliments but also encouragement regarding any recent places of growth and change that you have not recognized before. Learn how to speak blessings to one another, as we often read of people doing in the Bible. This gesture will always be humbling, will push back pride, and will create a "die to self" moment, when all focus is placed positively on the other person.

1. How did your affirmation and encouragement affect each other?

_____

_____

_____

_____

_____

_____

2. Was there anything shared that seemed to have a strong impact?

_____

_____

_____

_____

_____

_____

3. How might continuing to voice positives encourage a "living sacrifice" marriage?

_____

_____

_____

_____

_____

_____

IF YOU *THINK* A COMPLIMENT *OF* YOUR MATE, *SPEAK* THE COMPLIMENT *TO* YOUR MATE.

DAY 11

THE BLESSING OF BEING

See what great love the Father has lavished on us, that
we should be called children of God! And that is what
we are! The reason the world does not know us is that it
did not know him. Dear friends, now we are children of
God, and what we will be has not yet been made known.
But we know that when Christ appears, we shall be like
him, for we shall see him as he is.

1 John 3:1–2

The demands of busyness and frantic schedules flow into
every area of our lives. While most of us don't like this
lifestyle, we continue to run ourselves ragged, often feeling the
only solution is to speed up. There is no question that this constant push deeply affects our marriages. So that's the problem.
Today, let's look at an often-overlooked solution.

When you got engaged, there is a strong likelihood that at
some point you said something to your fiancé or fiancée such
as, "I cannot wait to be your husband," or "I cannot wait to be

your wife." No one says, "I can't wait to do husband [or wife] things." No, in the beginning we focus our attention on *being* married.

More often than not, marriage vows contain the words, "I take you to *be* my lawfully wedded husband/wife." Following the singular *be* comes the plural *dos*—do you promise . . . to have and to hold, to honor and cherish, and so on. But the *dos* only flow out of the *be*, not vice versa. Interesting that most of us began our marriages with this right perspective, even vowing to live this way, but then quickly became fixated on and addicted to the *dos*. And then, of course, the *don'ts* quickly follow and multiply.

In a culture that glorifies the quick fix, we must realize the main goal in a marriage is simply to be. While certainly we want to *do* something for our spouses to solve any short-term or long-term issues, job number one is to *be* there. The *do* puts pressure on us to find the right solution, while the *be* removes demand and expectation. This requires simple and intentional availability, as well as presence.

When asked about his success, a veteran elephant trainer stated, "They're extremely intelligent animals, so they catch on quickly to any training, but it's the relationship that takes time." This is a great truth and reminder for marriage—we may catch on quickly to marital "training"—the *dos*—but it's the "relationship"—the *be*—that takes time.

Today's scripture does not talk about what we must *do* to be God's children, but rather tells us what we already are in Christ. John encourages us to simply *be* who—and whose—we are.

Creating Connection

We all know the power of a compassionate look at the right moment, the reaching out of the hand at the perfect time, or the security and warmth of a much-needed embrace. Those can feel so right because they are all the gift of *being* a husband or wife, being available and present. In fact, those expressions of love so often come when we just don't know what to *do*. Share any moments like this that you recall in your relationship. Talk about the ministry of presence, of experiencing more of the *be* and less focus on the busyness of the *dos*. Decide together to find more expressions of your commitment to *be* a husband and wife.

1. How is so much focus on *doing* often a distraction from simply *being* married?

_____

_____

_____

_____

_____

_____

_____

2. How can not knowing what to do actually create the most loving expressions?

_____

_____

_____

_____

_____

3. How could better understanding this concept of *being* improve not only your marriage but also your walk with God?

_____

_____

_____

_____

_____

WHILE THE WORLD IS FOCUSED ON *DO*, KEEP YOUR EYES ON GOD'S *BE*.

DAY 12

MAKING ME-FOR-
YOU MOMENTS

The end of a matter is better than its beginning, and
patience is better than pride.

Ecclesiastes 7:8

Today's scripture is a powerful Bible verse for marriages that
are seeking to stop their me-against-you messes and create
more me-for-you moments. No matter how great your marriage
may be, as sinners, you will discover that irresponsibility, pas-
sivity, selfish demands, devaluing one another, and irrational
communication are going to be regular factors that impact the
relationship. Looking closely at these negatives, we see they are
all internal issues that rise up from our hearts and affect the
other person. Sometimes when one spouse engages in one of
these negatives, the other responds with another from this same
list. While we all know the old saying "Fight fire with fire," we
also know water is the best answer for putting out fires.

A powerful realization in relationships that actually is a sign of wisdom and maturity occurs when one spouse begins to manifest one of these negative behaviors, and the other starts looking for the external factor that might be causing the real problem. In other words, he or she chooses to bless instead of blame.

Just a few examples of these externals are job stress, financial demands, self-esteem struggles and insecurities, extended family interference and pressures, and conflicts with children, friends, neighbors, church members, and coworkers.

Could the short-tempered responses of late actually be an external issue being brought home? Could the silence in the evenings not need another "What's wrong with you tonight?" but instead a "Hey, I can tell something is going on. When you want to talk, I'm ready to listen"? In today's pressure-cooker culture, it is safe to say the majority of our internal strife that creates conflicts at home likely has its roots in a problem outside the four walls of home.

As sinners living with sinners, we are going to be in a continual battle with our internal and external issues. But through Christ, over time, we can grow and mature to decrease our negative response to them. Once we recognize an external issue, we can often find an immediate or certainly accelerated solution when we diagnose the origin and take action together as a couple. We must learn to fight outside forces together, not inside with each other.

Creating Connection

Let's create a mutual me-for-you moment. Think about each other's current stresses. What struggles do you know your spouse is experiencing right now? Consider what external factors may be impacting the situation. Have a proactive conversation, expressing understanding and compassion and asking each other about current stressors and what outside pressures may be weighing heavily. Your goal is not to "fix" anything but simply to listen and share the burden. Be sure, first, that you listen intently; then make certain that any words you speak bring benefit. Close by praying for each other.

1. What did you learn about external factors and how they impact your marriage?

   _____

   _____

   _____

   _____

   _____

   _____

   _____

   _____

2. What did you learn about internal factors and how they affect your marriage?

_____

_____

_____

_____

_____

_____

3. What was one valuable outcome from today's discussion with your spouse?

_____

_____

_____

_____

_____

_____

CHOOSE
TO BLESS,
NOT BLAME.

DAY 13

REDEEMING ROMANCE

Boaz replied, "I've been told all about what you have done for your mother-in-law since the death of your husband—how you left your father and mother and your homeland and came to live with a people you did not know before. May the LORD repay you for what you have done. May you be richly rewarded by the LORD, the God of Israel, under whose wings you have come to take refuge."

Ruth 2:11–12

One of the greatest love stories in the Bible is the account of Ruth and Boaz. And we should not miss the fact that despite the cultural norm of that day, God made sure the book in which this story appears was named after the woman in the story, not the man. This shows His heart toward the character, commitment, and compassion of this amazing woman.

Ruth stands out quickly as a widow who has decided to place the care of her mother-in-law, Naomi, first. A widow as well, Naomi has legally released Ruth from any family responsibility, but Ruth's commitment to her late husband and his family remains steadfast, regardless of their dire circumstances.

We are then introduced to Boaz, a wealthy, influential, and respected man in the community. He is a good man with a good name.

As Ruth goes out alone to try and gather food for herself and Naomi, she slips in behind the harvesters on Boaz's field to gather the grain left behind on the ground. When Boaz sees Ruth, rather than have someone chase her off, he goes to her personally to tell her to stay in his field only, instructing his workers to allow her in and even to share their food and water with her.

Ruth and Boaz were from completely different countries, backgrounds, and economic circumstances, but their character and common qualities drew them together. Their public reputations preceded them both. Boaz had already heard of Ruth's sacrifice and service to her husband's family. When he saw her in his field, he knew the kind of woman she was and blessed her for it. Throughout their short love story captured in Scripture, both of them proved again and again their loving commitment to God, others, and one another. Their like minds and hearts drew them together to fall in love and get married.

There is a popular saying that goes, "We become who we hang out with." Once we are married, this truth becomes ever so true in our relationship. This is exactly why our individual goals to consistently grow and mature in every way possible, especially spiritually, are so crucial.

Creating Connection

The book of Ruth is only four chapters long, yet it contains such an amazing, inspiring story of God leading people to discover great love. Take some time to read this book together in your favorite Bible translation. As you read, watch for and discuss the qualities of this couple that stand out to you. From this story, target at least one new area in your marriage in which you can grow together in godly reputation as well as in your relationship. Remember: the God of Ruth and Boaz is your God too.

1. What qualities stood out for you in Ruth? In Boaz?

_____

_____

_____

_____

_____

_____

2. What are specific ways you can work toward improving these qualities in your own lives and marriage?

_____

_____

_____

_____

_____

_____

3. What is one area in which you know God wants to grow the character of your marriage?

_____

_____

_____

_____

_____

GOD WANTS TO MAKE YOUR MARRIAGE INTO ONE OF THE GREATEST LOVE STORIES OF ALL TIME.

DAY 14

LOVE LETTERS

When Ruth came to her mother-in-law, Naomi asked,
"How did it go, my daughter?" Then she told her everything Boaz had done for her and added, "He gave me
these six measures of barley, saying, 'Don't go back to
your mother-in-law empty-handed.'" Then Naomi said,
"Wait, my daughter, until you find out what happens. For
the man will not rest until the matter is settled today."

Ruth 3:16–18

Today, we will once again look at the love story of Ruth and
Boaz from the book of Ruth.

In 1:16, Ruth tells Naomi, "Your God will be my God"
(NLT). We do not know Ruth's family background, but we must
assume that a part of her decision to stay with her mother-in-
law was due to her faith. We also see from Boaz's blessing of
Ruth in yesterday's passage that he was a man of God.

One of the most encouraging and inspiring aspects of the
book of Ruth is how hard this couple worked to do the right

thing before God and for one another. Their integrity prompted each to protect the other and their good names.

In chapter 3, Naomi told Ruth to go and visit Boaz at his threshing floor at night. She agreed. When Boaz woke up and realized she was there in recognition of who he was to her family, he immediately blessed her again and agreed to go through the proper channels to purchase and care for Naomi's estate as well as marry Ruth. They also agreed that she would leave early that morning, as nothing had occurred sexually between them, and they wanted to protect both their reputations, but especially Ruth's.

As we can see from today's scripture, after hearing the details of the night's conversation, Naomi basically told Ruth, "Just sit tight, honey. This guy won't stop until you are his." And she was right. The next day, Boaz did everything he'd promised he would do, even putting his love on the line to be certain that Ruth was provided with what was best for her. By the end of this romantic tale, they had become husband and wife, and it seems they really did live happily ever after. In fact, Ruth gave birth to a son named Obed, who became the grandfather of King David, which puts them in the family line of Jesus!

While the Bible has many stories of temptation, sin, and broken people making broken decisions who would then need God's rescue and redemption, right here in the middle of the Book is a story of two virtuous people who followed God from the beginning and handled their relationship with great care and integrity. What an inspiring story of love, faithfulness, and the great rewards for obedience to God.

Write out your own story, including the details of how you met, leading up to your love and marriage. Be sure to provide the particulars of how you felt, what you were drawn to in one another, and any key moments that convinced you that your spouse was "the one." You may each want to write your own version of the story, to present both sides. If so, when you are finished, take turns reading them. Also, writing and sharing your love story with the generations to come would make an amazing family heirloom.

1. Were there any surprising emotions or reactions while recalling and writing your story?

_____

_____

_____

_____

_____

2. Did writing your story reignite any old feelings as you reminisced?

_____

_____

_____

_____

_____

_____

3. How might having these letters strengthen your marriage and family in the future?

_____

_____

_____

_____

_____

_____

_____

GOD WANTS YOUR LOVE STORY TO BE AN INSPIRATION TO OTHERS.

DAY 15

THE LOVE TRIANGLE

"Truly I tell you, whatever you bind on earth will be bound in heaven, and whatever you loose on earth will be loosed in heaven. Again, truly I tell you that if two of you on earth agree about anything they ask for, it will be done for them by my Father in heaven. For where two or three gather in my name, there am I with them."

Matthew 18:18–20

From Darren's journal:

I believe serving here in Iraq as a chaplain is God's will for my life. Heather feels the same way. If she didn't feel the same, I wouldn't be doing this. The decision I made three years ago to pursue this ministry has finally panned out. While I didn't choose to go to war, I did choose to be in the Army and risk this possibility. Since that's the case, I'd rather be where God wants me than where I think it is best to be. My life is His, and I believe this is His plan for our marriage. It feels more right than anything I've ever done! I am blessed because I've found what I was made for! But Heather is the true hero of this story.

We all know how great life can be in a marriage when complete agreement comes on a major decision. Those times can be really exciting. We also know how tough things can get when a big disagreement brings a dark cloud over our marital sky. Agreeing or disagreeing, from the massive to the mundane issues in life, can become make-or-break moments in our relationships.

For the Christian couple, a spiritual dynamic exists when you decide together how life will be lived. We read about this overarching truth in today's passage as Jesus' words reveal a spirit-to-spirit agreement between God and His gathered people. This includes married couples.

Take a moment to draw a simple triangle. Write one of your names beside the left base angle and the other's name at the right base angle. Now, write "God" at the top point of your triangle. As you live out your relationship with God, you each move up your connecting sides toward Him. This not only moves you closer to Him but also simultaneously draws the two of you closer together. Even though Darren and Heather were thousands of miles apart, they were living in spiritual agreement together regarding his commitment in Iraq and her commitments in the United States.

The more marriage partners move toward God in agreement, the more unity will come. Conflicts and issues will arise, but if the big picture—the point of your life together—is always about God, He will lead and guide you both as one.

Share what you both feel to be your greatest point of agreement in life right now, a decision you have recently made that you both feel very good about. Where are you syncing really well and you both know and feel it? Take a few minutes to discuss how you found common ground to make that decision and agree. What steps did you take to best work together toward a solution? Use your triangle drawing as a visual motivation of how you can keep moving toward God together in other decisions and even in your conflicts. The bottom line—or baseline of your triangle—is you both want the best for your marriage, and so does God.

1. Was it encouraging to you both to consider how you reached your best decision lately? Why?

_____

_____

_____

_____

_____

_____

_____

2. How might discussing how you best came to a solution encourage you even in resolving conflict?

_____

_____

_____

_____

_____

_____

_____

ALWAYS KEEP
YOUR HOME
BUILT ON
COMMON GROUND.

REFINING THE
ROUGH EDGES

As iron sharpens iron, so one person sharpens another.

Proverbs 27:17

When we need to shine our silverware or buff a marble tabletop, we choose the softest polishing cloth we can find. The goal is to gently clean the delicate surface while taking great care to not scratch the finish. The end result is a brilliant shine. No grime. No scuffs. No marks. Just the brightest sheen possible.

When we want to refinish an antique table, a polishing cloth won't get the job done; instead, we need a piece of sandpaper. As we rub the surface, the grit will remove the outer finish that we no longer want to see so the new finish can be applied and adhere to add fresh beauty.

When thinking of your relationships, you could quickly write a list of the ones that "polish" you as well as the ones that "sand" you. We know the people in our lives who make us look good and feel great. But we also know the abrasive people who rub us the wrong way. We would all prefer to remove the sandpaper people from our lives and only keep the polishing people!

Often in marriage, the expectation is that we should just polish each other, but that is not only a false notion; it is also not at all fair. God's intention is for there to be plenty of times when we polish up and put the other mate proudly on display to look and feel awesome. But there are also just as many times when no one else in our lives can either see our rough edges or will tell us the truth about them. The person who can best see our blind spots and weak areas, the best one to gently tell us the truth about change, is our mate.

Do you think the "person" in today's verse is a polish cloth or a sandpaper relationship? Consider this: If you take two knives and use one to sharpen the other, you won't be polishing either of the blades, but you won't be hurting their finishes either. Yet both knives are sharpened in the process of rubbing the blades together.

Iron sharpening iron is a very fitting analogy for Christian marriage, even more than a polishing cloth and sandpaper. As you live in a relationship, you are both constantly sharpening the other by your daily interaction, communication, and even conflict.

So, thank God for your polishing friendships and your sandpaper relationships because He uses both to fashion you into the image of Christ. But the greatest and most impactful connection you have in your life is your spouse's "iron," constantly sharpening you.

Creating Connection

Using today's analogy, share with each other your number one polishing and sandpaper relationships outside your home. Talk through why these people affect you in this way and how God uses both to change you. Next, discuss the "iron sharpens iron" verse and how your own daily interaction sharpens you both, even in the tough moments of conflict. Close by being a polishing cloth to one another and share an encouraging word.

1. Did today's analogies help you better understand how God uses *all* relationships in your life? How?

_____

_____

_____

_____

_____

_____

_____

_____

_____

2. Did you and your spouse share any of the same "polishing" or "sanding" people? From what areas of life did your answers tend to come?

_____

_____

_____

_____

_____

3. How can the "iron sharpens iron" concept help you better understand conflict in your marriage?

_____

_____

_____

_____

_____

WHEN YOUR SPOUSE RUBS YOU THE WRONG WAY, THANK GOD FOR THE OPPORTUNITY TO BE SHARPENED.

Separating Saints from Sin

I have discovered this principle of life—that when I want to do what is right, I inevitably do what is wrong. I love God's law with all my heart. But there is another power within me that is at war with my mind. This power makes me a slave to the sin that is still within me. Oh, what a miserable person I am! Who will free me from this life that is dominated by sin and death? Thank God! The answer is in Jesus Christ our Lord. So you see how it is: In my mind I really want to obey God's law, but because of my sinful nature I am a slave to sin.

Romans 7:21–25 NLT

Kevin ran into an old friend, Brad, whom he hadn't seen in years. As they were quickly catching each other up on life, Kevin asked about Brad's wife. "So, how is Laura? You two doing well?" Brad smirked and said, "Well, we actually divorced a couple of years back." Kevin was surprised and responded, "Oh, man, I am so sorry. I had no idea." Brad laughed and said, "Don't be. She was crazy."

Laura, Brad's ex-wife, was at a sales conference for her job that she hadn't attended in a few years. She saw a colleague she recognized from the last time she had been at the event. After reviewing what had happened in the business, the friend asked Laura, "How is your husband? Brad, right?" Laura frowned, raised her eyebrows, and answered, "Yes, that's his name, but we divorced. It's fine, though; he was such a loser."

Unfortunately, these conversations go on in our culture on a regular basis. In reality, for so many such situations, quick but unfair sum-up words, like *crazy* and *loser*, are actually better interpreted as "I didn't understand how my spouse thought," "I lost patience with my spouse's emotions," "I didn't comprehend where my spouse was coming from in communication," or "I could never agree with how my spouse made decisions." These ignored and unresolved issues make harsh thoughts manifest long before the separation and disparaging words are actually spoken.

We can all too quickly write people off in relationships when miscommunication and misunderstandings consistently occur, regardless of fault. Based on the fact that we are all sinners, who demand our own way and will, we are often insecurity wrapped in self-absorption, yet with a deep desire to be heard and understood. As a bundle of unmet needs with a fear of the future, we can all get a little crazy, especially in a marriage, where you actually work hard to live in unity and community with each other.

As you can see from today's scripture, we are certainly in good company. Even the apostle Paul struggled with the pull of his humanity. His very honest confession came from not doing the right thing that he knew God wanted him to do, and on the flip side, also doing the wrong thing when he clearly knew the right way! But Paul's conclusion for himself is also our own, found in verse 25: "The answer is in Jesus Christ our Lord" (NLT).

The next time you have an argument and in your frustration are tempted to reduce your spouse to a single condescending word, go look in the mirror and remind yourself that your spouse married someone just as [fill in the blank] as you did.

Creating Connection

Following Paul's example from today's Bible passage, each of you share one thing in your life right now that you know is the right thing to do, but you are struggling to actually do it. Then each of you share something you are doing that you want to stop, but can't seem to find the strength. Close by encouraging and praying for one another in every area shared.

1. Did you have any common areas of struggle?

_____

_____

_____

_____

_____

_____

2. How might consistently sharing any shortcomings you want to overcome actually strengthen your marriage?

_____

_____

_____

_____

_____

3. How can regularly admitting faults *to* one another help you not find faults *in* one another?

_____

_____

_____

_____

_____

Confession is always a better choice than accusation.

DAY 18

PROBLEMS, PATTERNS, AND PROVIDENCE

The LORD gives wisdom; from his mouth come knowledge and understanding. He holds success in store for the upright, he is a shield to those whose walk is blameless, for he guards the course of the just and protects the way of his faithful ones. Then you will understand what is right and just and fair—every good path. For wisdom will enter your heart, and knowledge will be pleasant to your soul. Discretion will protect you, and understanding will guard you.

Proverbs 2:6-11

While we are certainly creatures of habit, we are also people of patterns—good and bad. And so many of us do not, maybe never in some cases, realize our own patterns by which we live. Identifying and becoming acutely aware of these can be a huge help in heading off problems in a marriage, from miscommunications to a crisis to a full-on meltdown.

Here are a few fictitious examples:

- *Incapacitating Problem 1:* "Every year, I seem to go through a short season of struggle in my marriage." *Identifying Pattern 1:* "I realized that in March, when I always enter into a difficult time and feel insecure, is when my first wife and I split up."
- *Incapacitating Problem 2:* "Every year, I battle deep depression for several weeks that is very trying for my marriage." *Identifying Pattern 2:* "My dad died in the same time frame as when I get depressed, and I have realized I never really dealt with his death."
- *Incapacitating Problem 3:* "Every year around Christmas and the New Year, I battle my self-worth and feel like a failure." *Identifying Pattern 3:* "Several years back, right around the holidays, I was let go from a company in which I had invested a lot of personal energy, and I still struggle with bitterness."

We can be completely puzzled by a very consistent pattern that we have created. But identifying this problem/pattern paradigm can help when we just don't understand why we do what we do on such a predictable basis.

One of the major growth points in marriage is when we can connect the dots of how we feel back to the root of what created those feelings to begin with. It takes great maturity and wisdom to discover the answer to the question, "Why do I do this?" But before delving into the past, the first question is, "Why do I have a pattern of feeling this way?"

One of God's great purposes in marriage is for a couple to encourage and help one another deal successfully with the past, tackle the present with passion, and press into the future with confidence. He made all the qualities in today's passage, such as honesty and integrity, available for you to receive from Him and give to each other. What a gift!

Creating Connection

Each of you think through at least one of your own individual recurring problems. Write down any thoughts that come to mind, if that helps. Use today's examples for a guide. The goal is simply to introduce this concept into your communication. Discuss how you can help each other identify patterns to ongoing problems. Lovingly process how this can be a helpful resource in your relationship, encouraging one another to make emotional and historical connections to improve the health of your lives and marriage.

1. Did anything that came up surprise either of you?

_____

_____

_____

_____

_____

_____

_____

2. Was there any revelation of a connection between a problem and a discovered pattern?

_____

_____

_____

_____

_____

3. How might you regularly use this resource together in the future?

_____

_____

_____

_____

_____

WISE CHOICES WILL WATCH OVER YOU, AND UNDERSTANDING WILL KEEP YOU SAFE.

DAY 19

PASSIONATE PARTNERSHIP

Place me like a seal over your heart, like a seal on your arm; for love is as strong as death, its jealousy unyielding as the grave. It burns like blazing fire, like a mighty flame. Many waters cannot quench love; rivers cannot sweep it away.

Song of Songs 8:6–7

Today, we're going to focus on three "-er" roles in marriage.

1. *Partner*

So often, when you hear someone from a lucrative business venture speak, you will hear the person begin with the phrase, "My partners and I . . ." We know this means that a small group of people decided to take a risk, divide responsibilities, and work as one to create a brand, product, or service that did not exist before. They fail together or they succeed together.

The people in a great business partnership seek to add

value to both the team and the outside world. They must constantly work together to be successful. In a marriage, these same factors are present. And while spouses are both certainly individuals, with their own minds and wills, it takes hard work to approach everything in life as one.

2. *Encourager*

The root word here is *courage*. An encourager literally speaks and acts to implant courage into hearts. While motivation from others outside the marriage is great and helpful, no one can deliver a strong dose of bravery quite like a spouse.

As needy humans, we consistently require physical, mental, emotional, and spiritual interaction to keep us moving forward in life. The longer we are married, the more we see that so many of the right decisions we have made are the sole result of the encouragement our spouses have provided. God is the Fuel, but our marriage is the vehicle He uses to carry us to our victories.

3. *Lover*

While this word seems to only have a sexual connotation in our culture, inside or outside of marriage, for the Christian, the greater context is that our spouses are the primary and sole human source for intimate love. Let's face it—we all love ourselves in unhealthy ways, but we can also hate ourselves, which is deadly. So, we deeply need a consistent and healthy outside source of love—one who will provide the proper perspective and the right place from whom true love can flow. This is why in the biblical context of marriage, sex becomes the icing on the cake, not the entire cake.

Today's scripture from the book of Song of Songs offers us great insight into a couple expressing their feelings toward being partners, encouragers, and lovers. An indivisible marriage maintains a solid partnership, uses encouragement to construct strong walls and a protective roof, while love decorates the home to make it beautiful inside and out.

Creating Connection

Pick out some passages from Song of Songs and take turns reading, switching back and forth according to your respective genders, focusing only on the verses where the two lovers speak. The entire book is only eight chapters, so if you have time, read them all. When you are finished, go back and reread any verses that could be used as encouragement for your partner. Feel free to improvise with your own poetic compliments as this Bible book inspires you.

1. How did these deeply intimate words from Scripture make you both feel?

_____

_____

_____

_____

_____

2. What do you think the inclusion of Song of Songs in the Bible could tell you both about what God wants for your own marriage?

_____

_____

_____

_____

_____

_____

3. How can you improve your level of encouragement toward one another?

_____

_____

_____

_____

_____

_____

FOR A FIRE TO KEEP BLAZING, THE FLAMES HAVE TO BE FED.

A LOVE LIKE THIS

Love is patient, love is kind and is not jealous; love does not brag and is not arrogant, does not act unbecomingly; it does not seek its own, is not provoked, does not take into account a wrong suffered, does not rejoice in unrighteousness, but rejoices with the truth; bears all things, believes all things, hopes all things, endures all things. Love never fails.

1 Corinthians 13:4–8 NASB

First Corinthians 13 in the Bible is likely the most read and well-known chapter in modern weddings. As a result, our church culture has deemed it "the love chapter." Paul's words are full of majesty and mystery as he describes the essence of what love means.

Who wouldn't want to be loved like this? Well, first the bad news. We are all incapable of fully loving to this degree in our sinful state. But the good news is, in Christ we have access to His perfect love to then be able to love others more fully.

One of the ways we can best grasp this truth is to replace

the word *love* with the name of Jesus in this passage, and suddenly, it all makes sense. When we know Christ and surrender our marriage to Him, we don't just know a loving God, but we may live from the very Source of love.

As Christian couples, we should exhibit a love that looks more like the description in today's passage than it does what the world reflects and defines as love. Christ's love should make our relationships appear and actually be markedly different. Consider these three ways His love creates this difference.

1. Christ's love gives us a *different place to look.*

    The hope of a future in heaven encourages us to keep looking forward and fix our eyes on Jesus, not on this world. For the Christian, the best really is yet to come.
2. Christ's love gives us a *different way to think.*

    Focusing on eternity creates a positive, optimistic, "glass half full" mind-set. The person with an attitude of hope not only will be a healthier person, but will also draw others to Christ by his or her very being.
3. Christ's love gives us a *different life to live.*

    We all desperately want to enjoy life. We want to feel contentment and live in the hope of a good day and a brighter tomorrow.

New life in Christ is not only a *different* way to live, but also the *best* way to live.

Here's a humbling but strong challenge you can use to test yourselves: Read today's passage, replacing the word *love* with your own names. As you read the words, think about your marriage. If one of the phrases feels good, then congratulations are in order. If one of them stings a bit, commit to doing some work on that area.

Creating Connection

Spend some time together viewing memories from your wedding ceremony by watching the recording, looking through photos, or even finding and reading your vows again. Taking each other back to reminisce about that special day can create an amazing, new moment in the present. Close by reading 1 Corinthians 13 together.

1. Was there anything that surprised you about recalling your wedding?

_____

_____

_____

_____

_____

2. What emotions did you feel from this experience?

_____

_____

_____

_____

_____

3. What is one area of life *today* that is better than you imagined it could be on your wedding day?

_____

_____

_____

_____

_____

_____

_____

LOVE NEVER GIVES UP, SO NEVER GIVE UP ON LOVE.

RESOLVE, RENEWAL, AND RENOVATION

Since God chose you to be the holy people he loves, you must clothe yourselves with tenderhearted mercy, kindness, humility, gentleness, and patience. Make allowance for each other's faults, and forgive anyone who offends you. Remember, the Lord forgave you, so you must forgive others. Above all, clothe yourselves with love, which binds us all together in perfect harmony.

Colossians 3:12–14 NLT

We all come into our marriages with some personal walls that we have built from hurts caused in the past by our families, friends, dating relationships, coworkers, fellow church members, and even enemies. When someone hurts us with words or actions or both, the natural defense is to create protection so this does not happen again.

To create a visual for the wall analogy, let's say we get hurt, so we grab an emotional "brick," and we set it out in front of us. We then get hurt in a much deeper way, and we gather several of these same bricks and start to stack them. If we choose not to deal with the hurts as they continue to come, we just keep stacking bricks, and eventually we build a wall around us so no one can get in to hurt us. Or so we think. If others are walled out, we are also walled in and isolated.

Even if we are completely sealed off emotionally, of course, people can still hurt us. So the reality is that we are hardening our hearts like the bricks. Every hurt just makes us harder but not stronger. We learn to detect the walls that others put up while unaware they can also detect ours. We can sense when someone is closed up emotionally and spiritually.

So we can come into our marriages with some bricks in place, or a partial wall built, or possibly for some, even a completely hardened fortress. But at the wedding altar, every brick we have in place makes for a blockage. This dynamic affects no other relationship as deeply as it does marriage. A partial wall already in place makes it so much easier to decide to add more bricks when marital issues arise. And the old saying is so true: hurting people hurt people.

In considering what God wants to build in our marriages, we must be honest about the walls that we have put up that are hurtful or damaging to our relationship—walls we must destroy or deconstruct as soon as possible. But that healing is exactly what Jesus is great at helping us do.

Each day we must make a choice to take bricks down to allow the other in, daily chipping away at our self-centered and self-preserving walls "with tenderhearted mercy, kindness, humility, gentleness, and patience." To have a growing, healthy relationship, to build an indivisible marriage, we have to choose to "make allowance for each other's faults, and forgive."

Find two small pieces of brick. If you don't have a brick, draw one on a piece of paper and tear it in half. As each of you holds a piece, agree together by God's grace, forgiveness, and mercy to start dismantling any walls between you, even if they were originally built from others' actions. Discuss any bricks that you know need to be taken down right away. Talk it out, and then forgive as today's passage clearly encourages. Keep the two pieces of brick where you both can see them to remind you of your commitment to deal with issues right away and so that forgiveness can keep the walls down and your hearts open to one another. More than anything, be open to what God wants to build with your marriage.

1. Did this discussion bring out any past issues?

_____

_____

_____

_____

_____

_____

_____

2. What about current issues?

_____

_____

_____

_____

_____

3. What steps can you continue to take to keep walls down?

_____

_____

_____

_____

_____

TEAR DOWN WALLS, AND BUILD EACH OTHER UP.

DAY 22

JEHOVAH IN THE HOUSE

"Now then," Joshua continued, "honor the LORD and serve him sincerely and faithfully. Get rid of the gods which your ancestors used to worship in Mesopotamia and in Egypt, and serve only the LORD. If you are not willing to serve him, decide today whom you will serve, the gods your ancestors worshiped in Mesopotamia or the gods of the Amorites, in whose land you are now living. As for my family and me, we will serve the LORD."

Joshua 24:14–15 GNT

In the early days of marriage, here are a few of the possible comments that can be heard expressed between a couple: "Well, I think we should spend Thanksgiving with my family. After all, it's a way bigger deal at my house." "At my family's, we always open one gift on Christmas Eve. How come your family doesn't do that?" "I don't want to go visit your parents on our vacation; I want us to do our own thing." One of the earliest issues in many marriages is dealing with the differences between and priorities of extended family.

Connected to this difficult dilemma is struggling with extended family dysfunction. Challenging communication styles, addictions, secrets, unfaithfulness, divisiveness, and betrayal are just a few of the major issues a marriage may have to deal with in one or both of the families you married into. Navigating these problems is going to be as customized as the family dynamics, with no one-size-fits-all solutions available. However, there is one decision you can make as a couple that will head off many issues, and you can find it in the book of Joshua.

Joshua, the leader of Israel, had gathered all the tribes together at Shechem. The goal was to present all the people to the Lord. Joshua had himself heard from God, so he spoke with boldness, reminding them all of Jehovah's great acts throughout their history, bringing them right up to their present day. He summed up his challenge from the Lord in the final line in verse 15 of today's scripture.

Joshua drew a "line in the sand" and told each family to choose a side. God or gods? Immanuel or idols? Time for each family to choose. Follow the disobedience of your ancestors or decide on obedience today? But he made it quite clear what his family's choice would be.

The very good news for your marriage is—whether one or both of you came from a horrible home, or from the perfect setting—you, as a married couple, get to choose your own direction. No matter if you came from dysfunction or from happily-ever-after, together you can choose to serve the Lord for the rest of your days together. In a very real way, Joshua shouted God's message out to the generations of the world and to every family.

Creating Connection

Each of you take turns sharing one thing you love about your own family and then one struggle you have. Openly discussing any family dynamics, both positive and negative, with one another can help each of you better identify with where you both have come from. These healthy conversations can also become points of understanding about where your own relationship needs to grow and mature as you both follow the Lord. Close this time by praying for both of your extended families and your own marriage.

1. Was sharing about your own families and your feelings helpful to one another?

_____

_____

_____

_____

_____

_____

_____

_____

2. Did this bring a better understanding of any extended family relationships? How?

_____

_____

_____

_____

_____

_____

3. How might this type of dialogue help you improve your own relationship?

_____

_____

_____

_____

_____

_____

NO MATTER WHERE YOU CAME FROM, GOD CAN GET YOU WHERE YOU NEED TO GO.

DAY 23

BATTLING BARRIERS

So he said to the paralyzed man, "I tell you, get up, take your mat and go home." Immediately he stood up in front of them, took what he had been lying on and went home praising God. Everyone was amazed and gave praise to God. They were filled with awe and said, "We have seen remarkable things today."

Luke 5:24–26

Jesus was in a home with so many people packed inside and gathered outside trying to get to Him that any access seemed hopeless. There were four friends who had carried their paralyzed buddy on a makeshift stretcher for Jesus to heal him. They arrived at the home, surveyed the standing-room-only crowd, and decided there was only one possible entry point left. Somehow they managed to get themselves and their friend up on the roof.

Next, they strategically began removing the roof tiles until they had cleared enough space to lower their friend's stretcher down to Jesus on ropes. Can you imagine being in that house when suddenly everyone starts feeling a draft, and then rays of sunlight beam in as a guy comes down on a mat?

When Jesus saw their ingenuity and obvious faith, He simply said, "Young man, your sins are forgiven" (v. 29 NLT). Instantly, the man was healed. Now, imagine being one of those four friends, holding that rope, looking down at what Jesus had done, realizing that exactly what you had all prayed and worked so hard to get had just happened?

Life's circumstances can bring incredible challenges. Oftentimes, when one mate is struggling, the other is available for support and added care. Even our marriage vows recognize these lows and the commitment required to see them through. There are going to be those days, weeks, months, and, in some cases, even years when a spouse is debilitated in some way through disease, illness, depression, anxiety, grief, or another struggle. In those seasons when we feel we don't know what else we can do, we must take the same course as these four friends: clear a path in life to place your mate before Jesus. Bypass all others in the way and remove all the barriers you can.

If you are walking through a hard season in your marriage, be encouraged today and allow your hope to be renewed. These men could have sat in their homes, hoping for some kind of miracle, but they decided to do whatever it took to place their friend before Jesus. You can do the same thing in the spiritual realm right now and in the days ahead. Don't give up. Don't let up. Don't quit. There will be a day you will be glad you persevered and pressed on.

Commit to praying regularly for each other. Not the generic "God bless our marriage" requests, but specific prayers, telling God in detail what you want to see happen in your marriage. Tell Him how you feel. Be honest. Be bold. Be blunt. He can handle whatever you need to express. Ask Him for favor and blessing as well as provision and protection. He wants your marriage to succeed, so partner with Him to that end when you pray. In time, you will start to see specific and miraculous answers to the time you invest bringing your marriage before Jesus.

1. What is the main difference in your prayers moving from general requests to specific intercession?

_____

_____

_____

_____

_____

_____

_____

_____

_____

2. How does being honest with God about your feelings regarding your marriage help you spiritually and emotionally?

_____

_____

_____

_____

_____

_____

_____

WHEN YOU DON'T KNOW WHAT TO DO OR WHERE TO TURN, GO STRAIGHT TO JESUS.

DAY 24

PERSONALIZING YOUR PERCEPTION

You will always harvest what you plant. Those who live only to satisfy their own sinful nature will harvest decay and death from that sinful nature. But those who live to please the Spirit will harvest everlasting life from the Spirit. So let's not get tired of doing what is good. At just the right time we will reap a harvest of blessing if we don't give up.

Galatians 6:7-9 NLT

A counselor could see that a husband had decided his marriage was over and was placing most of the blame on his wife. The doctor decided to employ a little reverse psychology on the man as a final try, believing that the couple had a great deal of potential for a healthy marriage.

After the husband asked for advice on how to break the news to his wife that night, the counselor asked if he would do him a favor. The man, grateful for the wisdom he had heard thus far, agreed. The doctor stated, "I want you to try an experiment for me even though I know you will hate this. For the next two weeks, no matter what your wife does, what she says, or how she acts, regardless of her behavior, I want you to love her, take care of her, compliment her, and do everything you can to make her feel secure in the relationship."

Confused, the man asked, "Why? Isn't that cruel when my plan is to ask for a divorce?"

The counselor answered, "Well, since you believe the demise of the marriage is her fault, use your last days together to show her what a great husband she's going to miss when you're gone."

Reluctantly, the man agreed to give it his best shot.

After two weeks passed, the husband came to his appointment. The doctor started first.

"Well, I'm sure life at home has been horrible, so let's talk about how to tell your wife about the divorce."

"Divorce!" the man shouted. "Why would I ever want to leave such a wonderful woman?! She has been absolutely amazing the past two weeks! I came to tell you I changed my mind; we are committed to working things out, and need your help."

The counselor's point: you do indeed reap what you sow.

Our *perspective* can be defined quite simply as the way we view something, while our *perception* is how we process what we view. A vital protective device for marriage is to constantly monitor both perspective and perception. So many outside factors can skew *what* we see and *how* we see, sneaking in to become detrimental in our most important relationship.

The husband in today's story desperately needed a new perspective on his marriage and a new perception of his wife. His intentional work on his own attitude and actions radically changed both. We must remind ourselves of Paul's words and apply them where they count the most—with our mates: "Let's not get tired of doing what is good. At just the right time we will reap a harvest of blessing if we don't give up."

Creating Connection

Most everyone loves receiving a gift card or a free coupon. Think of a few of each other's favorite simple pleasures, like a neck rub, a quiet dinner out, or the opportunity to sleep in on a Saturday. Create some simple, customized coupons with a matching message for each other. Maybe provide one every month this year. Let these be redeemed at will, with a little advance notice, and choose to make the blessing a great experience.

1. How did creating the coupons affect your perspectives?

_____

_____

_____

_____

_____

_____

2. Was this activity fun for you both? Why?

_____

_____

_____

_____

_____

_____

3. How do simple acts of love such as this create a positive spin on "reap and sow, plant and harvest"?

_____

_____

_____

_____

_____

_____

SEE YOURSELF THROUGH YOUR MATE'S EYES.

DAY 25

I GOT YOUR BACK

God, who said, "Let light shine out of darkness," made his light shine in our hearts to give us the light of the knowledge of God's glory displayed in the face of Christ. But we have this treasure in jars of clay to show that this all-surpassing power is from God and not from us. We are hard pressed on every side, but not crushed; perplexed, but not in despair; persecuted, but not abandoned; struck down, but not destroyed. We always carry around in our body the death of Jesus, so that the life of Jesus may also be revealed in our body.

2 Corinthians 4:6–10

From Heather's journal:

We hosted a grief support gathering for the families in our unit. Many of the ladies came, including some who had just found out about their loss. It was incredibly painful. Wives were asking questions, like if they would be able to see their husband's body before burial. It was painful to be a part of, but looking back, I'm thankful to have been there.

I was overwhelmed by seeing this for the first time, but watching the other wives who have been there before was amazing. Even though they were terribly sad, I saw them bravely rise to the occasion to comfort those who will one day be able to comfort others.

Darren has often described the soldiers as "tender warriors." I must say that these women are tender warriors themselves. Tender to comfort the hurting and care for their families, and warriors to stand in the face of fear, sorrow, loss, loneliness, and exhaustion. It doesn't make sense, but there is nowhere I would rather be right now. In this place, there is nowhere to get comfort and peace other than Christ. Pray that we all run to Him.

The problems and struggles in our modern culture are often overwhelming to us. Knowing we can stand back-to-back with our mates and trust that we will battle the world together is such an important aspect of marriage. Today's passage encourages us that although we are "hard pressed on every side," "perplexed," and even "persecuted" or "struck down," Christ's life is available, alive in us, and "his light [will] shine in our hearts."

Darren and Heather's term for soldiers is actually a great description of the partners in a Christian marriage—"tender warriors"—spouses who are "tender to comfort the hurting and care for their families, and warriors to stand in the face of fear, sorrow, loss, loneliness, and exhaustion." Isn't it wonderful that "there is nowhere you would rather be" than facing the world together with your mate, knowing "there is nowhere to get comfort and peace other than Christ" as together, you "run to Him"?

Creating Connection

We all know the phrase "I've got your back." Those words are always so welcome and comforting to hear when you are struggling with life. Share with one another ways you need the other to be a "tender warrior" today on your behalf—to pray, support, and serve. Share your burdens, cares, and hurts. Ask one another, "Is there any specific way I can fight for you today?" Then back up what is spoken with your actions.

1. How could this mind-set create more back-to-back support and less in-your-face conflict?

_____

_____

_____

_____

_____

_____

2. Were either of you relieved by sharing burdens or the offer of support?

_____

_____

_____

_____

_____

3. Is there any specific action you should continue to take to fight for one another?

_____

_____

_____

_____

_____

BE A TENDER WARRIOR AND FIGHT BESIDE YOUR MATE FOR YOUR MARRIAGE.

FIREPLACES AND WILDFIRES

"You know the next commandment pretty well, too:
'Don't go to bed with another's spouse.' But don't think
you've preserved your virtue simply by staying out of
bed. Your *heart* can be corrupted by lust even quicker
than your *body*. Those leering looks you think nobody
notices—they also corrupt."

Matthew 5:27-28 MSG

When God gave Moses the Ten Commandments, they offered amazing insight into what He values. After all, He could have given one hundred laws, one thousand laws, or any vast number, but He gave only ten. Of those, four have to do with our vertical relationship with Him, and the remaining six have to do with our horizontal relationships with others. But every single commandment is about a relationship, nothing else.

Two of the ten speak directly to protecting the marriage relationship. This was an early indicator of God's priority of this covenant relationship that He had created and ordained for all time. Throughout Jesus' ministry, He continually connected to the entire Old Testament, but most especially to Moses. In one particular setting when discussing marriage and commandments, He gave a deeper and broader perspective of God's heart for the sanctity and purity of the marital commitment. In today's scripture, Christ reminds us that our hearts can be corrupted even quicker than our bodies can.

Regardless of age or stage in life, we would all agree that we live in a sex-infused society today. A newscast that doesn't include something sexual is rare. The issue with impurity is rampant. But this pervasive problem is nothing new. That is exactly why Jesus expanded on the true concept behind the commandment and why we must pay close attention to His words.

A helpful analogy is to think of marital sex as the fireplace in the house. Nowhere else in the home is it safe to build a fire except for the fireplace; hence, the name. Anywhere else in the home where a large, open flame is introduced can burn down the entire structure, and the family will lose everything.

Every year in California, the news broadcasts images of dry conditions and strong winds coupled with a careless person's actions where a wildfire has been created and spreads destruction in its wake.

Sex, like fire, can be an amazing and life-giving element when it occurs in its God-given place, but light a fire anywhere else, and people get burned. We see this over and again. We must keep in mind that God created sex for our good and His glory, which is exactly why from Moses to Jesus to today, we must listen to His words and obey His instruction to have the best relationship of intimacy in marriage we possibly can.

Sex can sometimes be a difficult topic to discuss, even in the best of marriages. That is exactly why it is one of the most prevalent issues inside counselors' offices. But relational health is best maintained as well as grown in open and honest communication. Is there any aspect of your intimate relationship the two of you need to discuss? Is there anywhere either of you need to biblically protect your relationship? Maybe the answer to these questions is yes, but each of you has different concerns. Consider connecting your discussions to specific scripture, like today's. Don't be afraid or shy about bringing up a topic in your marriage to which the Bible clearly does not hesitate to directly and honestly speak.

1. Are you both able to discuss sex within a biblical context? Why or why not?

_____

_____

_____

_____

_____

_____

_____

2. What concerns came up that were the same and which were different?

_____

_____

_____

_____

_____

3. Were you able to connect and resolve any concerns? Why or why not?

_____

_____

_____

_____

_____

GOD CREATED SEX INSIDE MARRIAGE FOR OUR GOOD AND HIS GLORY.

DAY 27

MAXIMIZING MATURITY

Just as you received Christ Jesus as Lord, continue to
live your lives in him, rooted and built up in him, strengthened in the faith as you were taught, and overflowing
with thankfulness.

Colossians 2:6–7

Most people do not get through childhood without experiencing the joy and tragedy of owning a goldfish. Joy
because they are fun to watch swim around and explore, and
tragedy because they quite often die all too soon. But God
placed an interesting survival characteristic in goldfish that
makes them unique.

This species of fish will grow to the size that their environment can sustain and then will stop. But if introduced into a
larger setting, the goldfish will start to grow again until once
again reaching its instinctive maximum size. It is not unusual
to hear reports from people who upgrade their aquariums that
their goldfish will increase in size every time the environment is

made larger. Most of the deer species in the United States have this same characteristic. That is why when you see construction and civilization encroaching on a forested area, people also begin to notice the physical size of the deer in the area becoming smaller.

As Christians, we are just like the goldfish and the deer in our spiritual state. We will only grow to the size that our environment allows, and then we will stop or stagnate. But if a new catalyst is introduced, such as a discipleship opportunity or some other inspiration or challenge to grow, we will begin to mature again. This places the responsibility to stay in a nurturing spiritual environment squarely on our own shoulders. The challenge of continual growth and maturity was present throughout all of Paul's letters, as we read in today's scripture.

Paul's words are very intentional: "received," "continue," "rooted," "built up," "strengthened," and "overflowing"—all proactive words with a definite progression from the inside out, from roots to fruit.

In your marriage, have you ever considered that you have a responsibility toward the spiritual growth of your spouse? While we will never be accountable for each other's individual actions or sin, we are accountable to one another in our walk with God. Whether you were both Christ-followers when you got married or have come into a relationship with Him since your wedding, His intention is that you continually inspire, encourage, and accelerate each other's spiritual growth and maturity. You can both be stronger believers because you are in each other's lives. You can do far more together for Him than you ever would have been able to do alone. That is part of His great purpose in bringing you together in this life.

If you do not regularly read God's Word together, or if it has been a very long time, now is a great opportunity to engage or reengage. A strong plan is to start at the first of a month and each day, read a chapter together from Proverbs (thirty-one chapters). You can also start in Matthew and work your way through the Gospels. Reading Scripture together through the lens of your marriage can be a unique and deeply personal experience as a couple. And you will most certainly grow in maturity together as you read and discuss your daily passage.

1. Is making a mutually spiritual commitment difficult? Why or why not?

_____

_____

_____

_____

_____

_____

_____

_____

2. What benefits could come from this commitment to read together and grow together?

_____

_____

_____

_____

_____

_____

3. How might God change your marriage through the reading of His Word?

_____

_____

_____

_____

_____

DEEPEN YOUR ROOTS AND GOD WILL GROW YOUR FRUIT.

DAY 28

PREEXISTING CONDITIONS

Principled people hold tight, keep a firm grip on life,
sure that their clean, pure hands will get stronger and
stronger!

Job 17:9 MSG

A secret weapon that many successful Christian marriages use regularly and frequently is a set of principles. For Christians, a *principle* is a self-imposed, predetermined guideline based on Scripture by which you commit to abide. These can be short-term to solve a temporary issue or long-term for consistent protection or provision. A principle is not a rule or a law, but an intentional commitment to a growth plan. Just as you may shower daily at a certain time without even thinking about it, a principle becomes an automatic habitual decision for your good. If you began a pattern years ago of showering every morning or bathing each night, rarely do you deviate from that plan. You don't decide each time; you just do it.

Setting a principle is making a decision about what your

actions or reactions will be *before* you are placed in the situation. A principle can help you create an opportunity as well as avoid a circumstance. Mistakes are often made when we are put in the position to make impulsive choices. Problems come when we do something again that we hated doing the last time. Waiting to make a decision until you face a temptation, dilemma, or even an aggravation can often lead to a wrong or simply regrettable choice. Establishing some simple principles can help you avoid these situations completely.

For a married couple, here are a few examples of protective principles:

- I will not connect with anyone of the opposite sex on social media without my spouse being aware of and in agreement with it.
- I will not meet with or ride with someone of the opposite sex alone without my spouse being aware of and in agreement with the situation.
- I will allow my spouse access to my phone, tablet, and computer for accountability.

Here are a few examples of provisional principles:

- Aside from sickness or unavoidable work schedules, we will go to church together weekly.
- We will pray together regularly on a mutually agreed-upon schedule.
- Once a week, we will share how we are growing or struggling in our spiritual lives.

Likely you can think of at least one marriage, if not more, that might have been saved if just one of these principles had been adopted earlier in their relationship. You never know when enacting some proactive measure might actually save your own marriage now from a problem coming down the road.

Creating Connection

Discuss the concept of principles together for full understanding. Honest talks like this that are safe from arguments or accusations can open up concerns that have been brewing for a while. That is the point of principles. Spend some time thinking through both provisional and protective principles. Write down anything you both agree to begin, then periodically discuss your progress. Be certain to talk about any problems or issues that get solved or subverted by your decision to be proactive in your marriage.

1. Was this discussion difficult or a relief in some area that needed to be addressed?

   _____

   _____

   _____

   _____

   _____

   _____

2. How do you plan on following up on any principles that you established?

_____

_____

_____

_____

_____

_____

3. Do you think adding principles to your life can become a long-term pattern for you both? Why or why not?

_____

_____

_____

_____

_____

_____

PRINCIPLES PROVIDE PROVISION AND PROTECTION.

DAY 29

COMMITTED TO THE CLIMB

Two people are better off than one, for they can help each other succeed. If one person falls, the other can reach out and help. But someone who falls alone is in real trouble. Likewise, two people lying close together can keep each other warm. But how can one be warm alone? A person standing alone can be attacked and defeated, but two can stand back-to-back and conquer. Three are even better, for a triple-braided cord is not easily broken.

Ecclesiastes 4:9–12 NLT

Mountain climbing, rock climbing, and rappelling have become enormously popular sports in the past few years, attracting more and more athletes who spend millions of dollars on gear and trips to famous locations around the world.

While solo climbing is popular, many enthusiasts approach this activity as a team sport. The ability to work together and accomplish a feat, such as reaching the pinnacle of a mountain, inside the dynamics of a group is exhilarating. Another major factor is the safety and security of being connected and available to one another during the climb. Staying tethered can quite literally save someone from falling to his or her death after a simple misstep or slip of the hand.

Today's scripture helps us fully understand the power of helping one another up, physically and emotionally; the beauty of walking together when we have troubles; keeping warm on a frigid night, in reality or metaphorically; standing as one to face victories and valleys.

The "triple-braided cord" analogy comes alive when we realize what is holding us together individually and as a couple is Jesus Christ. He alone can help us be "not easily broken" in our marriages.

Life can certainly feel like a daily climb up a steep, sheer cliff. Being totally transparent about where you are in your marriage right now, how taut is the "cord" that is tethering you together spiritually? Is one of you much stronger than the other, so that the strain is starting to cause the other to struggle too? Has one fallen and the other is doing all he or she can to hold both up? So often in life, one is strong when the other is weak, but then there are those times when both feel as though they are about to fall to their deaths.

Please know that no matter the strength of either of you, the "triple-braided cord" is truly your constant answer. Christ is the third strand in your marriage and relationship, wrapping you in His safety and security. He can hold you both up and keep you from falling. The very difficult request that He often makes is that you both let go and fall to Him. But He will catch you every time. His climbing record is perfect, and He's never lost a team member yet!

Discuss the mountain-climbing analogy. Write down the strong and weak areas you both are facing right now. Talk about how to help and pull each other up. Next, write down the names of the people in your life to whom you know you are "tethered." Who can you truly trust? Who would reach out to catch you as a couple if you fell? Thank God for those relationships, and pray for each other's strengths and weaknesses as you fall together toward the One who can always catch you.

1. Was it difficult to discuss and admit weak as well as strong areas of life? Why or why not?

_____

_____

_____

_____

_____

_____

_____

_____

_____

_____

2. Were you in agreement with your tethered relationships, or did any surprise you?

_____

_____

_____

_____

_____

3. How can you best keep reminding and encouraging one another that you are wrapped in a "triple-braided cord" with Christ?

_____

_____

_____

_____

_____

CLIMB COURAGEOUSLY, COUPLED AND CONNECTED TO CHRIST.

DAY 30

REACHING OUT,
GROWING DEEP

I pray that out of his glorious riches he may strengthen
you with power through his Spirit in your inner being,
so that Christ may dwell in your hearts through faith.
And I pray that you, being rooted and established in
love, may have power, together with all the Lord's holy
people, to grasp how wide and long and high and deep
is the love of Christ, and to know this love that surpasses
knowledge—that you may be filled to the measure of all
the fullness of God.

Ephesians 3:16–19

Counted among the largest living things on earth are the
giant sequoia trees found in Northern California. These
massive trees cover more than thirty-five thousand acres of forest. Some of them measure more than three hundred feet tall
and boast trunks as large as forty feet in diameter. Many of

these trees are calculated to be two thousand to three thousand years old.

While massive oak trees, for example, are often seen standing alone, sequoias are always found close together. The oak tree's roots go down very deep to anchor and sustain the tree by itself, while the sequoias' root system is very shallow, often only going down twelve to fifteen feet. The difference for these giants of the forest is that their roots extend out to reach far distances.

Giant sequoias maintain their massive growth by:

- fusing their root systems together
- sharing their resources
- cooperating rather than competing with one another for their existence

Sequoias' roots wrap around and support each other, which has proven to be much stronger than if they went very deep by themselves. Because of this dynamic, they also overcome many of the natural challenges of drought, fire, disease, and insects that kill other forest trees.[1]

When we were single, like the lone oak tree, we had no choice but to try and grow our roots deep to anchor ourselves alone. But regardless of how deep those roots were, upon our wedding day we must take on the nature of the sequoia, reaching out to fuse our roots together, sharing resources, and cooperating, not competing. Depending on how long a person was single or the level of his or her independence, this can be a true challenge for many in marriage. There is also often a connection between how much we are willing to intertwine our roots with our spouses' and our ability to allow our hearts to be grounded in God, as today's scripture encourages.

How extensively are your roots intertwined in your marriage? Do you share individual resources to accomplish what is best for you both in the relationship? Is there any area where you need to focus on cooperating and not competing? These are valuable questions to honestly answer for those who desire to not only deepen their roots together but also grow strong and mature as a couple, reaching their full potential in life.

Creating Connection

Work through the questions in the previous paragraph. Focus on places in your relationship where you can fuse together even more than you have already. Discuss how you can maximize the potential of all the gifts and skills in you both. What steps can you take or increase in consistency in your spiritual growth so that you can "be made complete with all the fullness of life and power that comes from God" (v. 19 NLT)?

1. Did you determine any individual resources that you have yet to share?

_____

_____

_____

_____

_____

2. Was there any area where you have been competing and not cooperating?

_____

_____

_____

_____

_____

3. Did you identify anywhere your spiritual roots can more closely intertwine?

_____

_____

_____

_____

_____

WRAP YOUR ROOTS AND SHARE YOUR RESOURCES.

DAY 31

GETTING THE GOOD GIFTS

Homes are built on the foundation of wisdom and understanding. Where there is knowledge, the rooms are fur-
nished with valuable, beautiful things. Being wise is better than being strong; yes, knowledge is more important
than strength.

Proverbs 24:3–5 GNT

One of the most fun activities an engaged couple is privi-
leged to do as they head toward their wedding day is to
create the "wish list" for the showers people will host for them.
A couple decides the retail or online stores where they want to
register and then select or scan the various household items they
hope to have. The invited guests can then view their list and buy
an item they know the couple desires to place in their home.

Finally, the day arrives when the wedding is over, the couple
is married and moved into their first home, and the gifts are
all opened. Next, they will spend many hours deciding how to
configure the kitchen gadgets and dishware into drawers and

cabinets, while finding the perfect spots on the walls to hang their new decorations. Once every box is emptied and every item is put into place, there is an amazing sense of satisfaction and security that the newlywed husband and wife experience regarding their life together. Everything in its place and a place for everything feels really good.

As the years pass, problems arise, struggles come, and challenging days arrive, there is often a new realization of a very different type of need and desire for the couple in their home. These are gifts that no one can see, that can't be stored or hung or even purchased. Life demands some internal decoration, so to speak, to be able to deal with everything that comes their way.

The decorations in our home are enjoyable to us and anyone who may visit, but as we see in today's scripture, when we begin to attain wisdom, understanding, and knowledge, these will benefit not only us but all those with whom we come into contact. James 1:5 states, "If you need wisdom, ask our generous God, and he will give it to you. He will not rebuke you for asking" (NLT). We can read, study, and scour the internet for knowledge in many areas, including spiritual, which can certainly provide us with information, but true wisdom only comes from engaging in a relationship with God.

Are you at a stage in life or at a difficult place where wisdom is much more of a need than a new decoration? Understanding and knowledge would make a lot more sense to add than a new piece of furniture. The great news is, God promises you can go to Him to build your "house" in His ways.

Decide today to regularly pray for wisdom in your lives and marriage. Ask your generous God, who promises to deliver directly to both of you. Go ahead and add knowledge and good sense to your prayer if you like. Digging deeper into God's Word will also be a strong support to your prayers. Searching and finding the many verses on wisdom in the book of Proverbs will help you furnish your home with God's blessings. Pay close attention in the days ahead as He delivers on His promise to you both.

1. Why do you suppose gaining wisdom is such a different process from getting knowledge?

_____

_____

_____

_____

_____

_____

_____

_____

_____

2. What are some ways you can ensure you will keep asking God for wisdom over the long haul?

_____

_____

_____

_____

_____

_____

3. Can you think of a time when you know you received God's wisdom?

_____

_____

_____

_____

_____

_____

WEALTH WILL EVENTUALLY BURN, BUT WISDOM WILL ALWAYS BENEFIT.

DAY 32

A COMPLEMENTING COMBINATION

We know that in all things God works for the good of those who love him, who have been called according to his purpose.

Romans 8:28

Unfortunately, in these volatile times in which we live, we have all witnessed marriages implode, causing those families to explode. A private disintegration for a couple within the walls of a home eventually becomes public knowledge when the two divide. So how can we address sooner in marriage what always starts out small but slowly grows into a giant issue? And what if those dynamics of destruction could be healed and harnessed for good before the relational fuse is lit?

Nitrogen is a colorless and odorless gas used to make fertilizers, nitric acid, and dyes.[2] Glycerin is a colorless and odorless syrupy, sweet liquid used to make cosmetics, perfumes, and medicines.[3] Nitrogen and glycerin by themselves are not dangerous. But when combined together—made *one*, if you will—they are quite deadly in an explosive device. United, they become an entirely different force that requires a completely new level of care, attention, and respect.

During the 1860s, Alfred Nobel, the namesake of the Nobel Peace prize, developed the manufacturing of nitroglycerin, which became revolutionary in mining and construction for blasting tunnels, cutting canals, and clearing paths through the landscape to build railways and roads. Therefore, the original intent and primary use of Nobel's harnessing of the power of these two elements for explosion was not for destruction or harm, but for construction and humankind's benefit.[4]

In all marriages, the same dynamics that can create division and destruction can be turned around and utilized for adding benefit and blessing to the relationship. Fiery passion, for example, can make for horrible fights but can also be harnessed to work together with amazing energy. Strong individual wills can create stubborn standoffs but can also fuel great tandem tenacity to never give up.

When a couple gives all their strengths and weaknesses to God, their marriage can become like nitroglycerin—with an explosive power to do good together and for His glory.

When God wills for a couple to commit to a lifelong marriage as one in Him, He is combining an explosive force in the world and His kingdom to bless the couple, benefit others' lives, and literally change the world together.

Today's scripture is an often-quoted and familiar verse, and we need to be sure that we connect its words to marriage for encouragement and as a reminder that God can work *everything* together for our good. The very things that trigger explosions in our relationships can be harnessed and used for extraordinary purposes, if we will allow God to work for good as He has called us to Him.

1. Was it easy or difficult to discover these "nitroglycerin" areas of your marriage?

_____

_____

_____

_____

_____

_____

2. Did anyone else reveal a combined strength that you didn't realize before?

_____

_____

_____

_____

_____

3. What are some ways you can maximize your marital "nitroglycerin"?

_____

_____

_____

_____

_____

GOD WILL WORK FOR YOUR GOOD AS YOU DO WHAT IS BEST FOR ONE ANOTHER.

DAY 33

EXITING BAGGAGE CLAIM

Then Peter came to Jesus and asked, "Lord, how many times shall I forgive my brother or sister who sins against me? Up to seven times?" Jesus answered, "I tell you, not seven times, but seventy-seven times.

Matthew 18:21–22

One of the major points of contention when a couple takes any sort of trip can be the amount of luggage or bags brought along. A romantic getaway can begin with an argument in the driveway over the number of suitcases required. From "Why do you need a bag just for shoes?" to "What are you thinking, bringing your golf clubs this weekend?" the expectation and perception of excess baggage can quickly create conflict.

As we well know, there is a very different type of baggage in a marriage. While we can't necessarily see it, we know it exists, especially when opened up and unpacked in a heated moment. But we all bring emotional baggage from our past into the marriage relationship. We can try very hard to work it out as much as possible during dating and engagement, but some things just do not surface until a couple lives together on a daily basis.

Premarital counseling is a wonderful resource, but so often at that stage, couples are only seeing the best in one another and pushing aside any issues. Only when competing for first place in the shower in the morning, looking over a credit card bill together, or realizing there's a habit of which we were not previously aware will unseen baggage become glaringly visible.

Today's scripture talks about the need to forgive others over and over. Jesus often used obvious exaggeration as a method of teaching truths. He was not telling His disciples that on the 491st occasion of an offense, you then had the right to choose bitterness and resentment. In fact, His words mean, essentially, to lose count; don't count at all; let it go.

While Jesus intended this principle for all relationships in the Christian's life, nowhere is it more crucial than in marriage. If heeded, these two verses alone could save countless relationships. To be clear, Jesus did not say that you shouldn't notice the offense or you should ignore that it happened, but rather to make forgiveness your default response.

Isn't it amazing that none of us ever go to Jesus following a sin, ask Him for forgiveness, only to hear Him say, "Well, I'm sorry, but no. You have reached your sin quota, so I cannot forgive you." Thank God that never occurs. Why? Because He is "not counting people's sins against them," as 2 Corinthians 5:19 states.

In your marriage, do you have a baggage limit? Do you keep a tally on sin? Maintaining a short list with a short memory regarding offenses in marriage is a right and healthy choice. And the Bible commands us to forgive as Christ forgives (Ephesians 4:32), which means to stop counting.

Creating Connection

In your own marriage, learn to realize and watch for any time when outside help is needed to deal with recurring and debilitating issues. There should be no hesitancy in getting counseling for your marriage. If you realize some baggage is overwhelming your relationship and solutions are elusive, talk to your pastor or seek out a marital counselor. Answers are available, and often within just one or two sessions with the right professional, your growth can accelerate as a couple into the place you desire and deserve.

1. Is the baggage in your marriage easily identifiable or more like an invisible destructive force?

_____

_____

_____

_____

_____

_____

_____

_____

2. Are both of you open to getting help when needed? If not, why?

_____

_____

_____

_____

_____

_____

3. Imagine your marriage without the issue that is weighing on you most today. What steps can you take to work toward victory?

_____

_____

_____

_____

_____

_____

LET GO
AND LOVE.

DAY 34

ASSERTIVE ACCEPTANCE

We know and rely on the love God has for us. God is love. Whoever lives in love lives in God, and God in them. This is how love is made complete among us so that we will have confidence on the day of judgment: In this world we are like Jesus. There is no fear in love. But perfect love drives out fear, because fear has to do with punishment. The one who fears is not made perfect in love. We love because he first loved us.

1 John 4:16–19

Picture a chameleon. Yes, the slow-moving, bug-eyed, lime-green lizards. The key characteristic of this reptile is that many of the species can instinctively adapt the color of their skin to their background or environment to disguise themselves and hide from predators. Turning pink, blue, brown, black, yellow, or purple? No problem. The lizard can adapt and fit right in.

As people, also often insecure and uncertain of our

environments, we obviously can't change colors, but we can alter our personalities to suit our current setting.

For example, a typically introverted man sees that the managers at his new job joke a lot, sometimes excessively, even inappropriately at times. Looking for acceptance and promotion, he works hard to be a comedian in that setting. The problem comes when he realizes he can't keep up the charade of presenting a false front.

A woman, normally very outgoing, begins to connect with a group at her new church that tends to be very subdued and far too stoic for her taste. But desiring to fit in there, she constantly bites her tongue and silences her usual verbal flair. The problem comes when they finally accept her, she doesn't like who she has become for them.

We should never work to become someone we are not. This is especially detrimental when people have never seen who we truly are and therefore cannot know us. The chameleon lifestyle is exhausting and dangerous, to the point that we can start to wonder who we are anymore.

The best place to kill the chameleon is within marriage.

In our relationships, when we allow ourselves to be fully known and receive acceptance, holding back no aspect of our personalities from one another, this can build a secure foundation for every area of life. If at the core of who we are in the most intimate relationship we have, we believe we are good enough and there is grace for the rest, then we can be ourselves in any setting. This is one of the greatest gifts a couple can give each other.

As you read in today's scripture, God accepts us just as we are. We don't have to "get our act together" first for His love to live in our hearts. Fear and judgment in our culture create social chameleons. The love of God and our mates cultivates trust, love, and confidence. Our marriage in and through Christ can be a reflection of that love.

Creating Connection

Discuss the chameleon syndrome. Walk through your circles of influence and identify anywhere either of you are tempted to change who you are. Talk about why you feel this way. Encourage one another in who you are, and remind each other that you are indeed good enough for every single setting because it is exactly that way at home in your love. Should there be any areas within your marriage where there is discomfort in identity, talk openly and gracefully about those feelings to address needed change.

1. Did you identify chameleon areas in your lives? What were they?

_____

_____

_____

_____

_____

_____

_____

2. What changes will you make as a result?

_____

_____

_____

_____

_____

_____

3. How did this conversation encourage you both in your identities?

_____

_____

_____

_____

_____

_____

DON'T CHANGE WHO YOU ARE IN THE WORLD. CHANGE THE WORLD WITH WHO YOU ARE.

DAY 35

YOUR MARRIAGE MISSION

We are therefore Christ's ambassadors, as though God
were making his appeal through us. We implore you on
Christ's behalf: Be reconciled to God. God made him
who had no sin to be sin for us, so that in him we might
become the righteousness of God.

2 Corinthians 5:20–21

From Darren's journal:

*I was told that deployments strengthen strong mar-
riages and weaken weak marriages. That is the truth!
I miss Heather now more than I ever have, and when
we've talked on the phone, I can "hear" her smile. I am
thankful for our marriage. But there are lots of guys
here who are already mad at their wives and vice versa.
It's sad to watch.*

*One of my soldiers is already thinking about fil-
ing for divorce from over here. How miserable would*

that be! Pray for not only his marriage to heal but for his focus to get straight, or he will become a liability. Strong families make strong soldiers.

That is one of the missions of a chaplain: to encourage soldiers to care for their families even from here, and many times, for me to show them by loving my family in front of them. A lot of them have never seen a healthy family unit. I pray they see that in mine.

Regardless of your background, age, or life experience, the trials of life will "strengthen strong marriages and weaken weak marriages." Relationships are like plants—always either growing or dying. There is no neutral zone where a plant exists in a static state. Most of the time you can look at the leaves and their colors to tell a plant's condition, but not always. There are times when a plant is in trouble but the signs are not yet obvious.

Likewise, every marriage is also either growing or dying. When our most important relationship in life is struggling, everything else is not quite right. If we don't get our focus straight, we can become a liability in the other areas of life. Why? Because we become distracted and troubled. Strong families make not only strong soldiers, but strong doctors, clerks, lawyers, sanitation workers, homemakers, realtors—you name it. No matter the job, the health and strength of our marriages and families make us or break us in the rest of life.

One of God's intentions for the Christian marriage is to do exactly what Darren stated regarding the witness to his soldiers. God wants our marriages to be examples to a lost and broken world of His life and work in the human race. We, too, are broken, but Christ makes the difference, and that change needs to be on display. None of us will ever be perfect, but we can represent our God as the answer to our imperfections. So many today have "never seen a healthy family unit," so let's work to make sure they see one in each of ours through Christ.

Creating Connection

Imagine for a moment that God called you as a couple to the mission field. What would be your response? Well, He actually already has. He wants to use you both in all your circles of influence. Discuss together how the two of you are Christ's ambassadors now. Where is He at work today in and around your lives? Where has He used you in the past? Where do you believe He still wants to take you but circumstances have not yet worked out? Discuss your marriage's "mission field" and how you can better position your-selves for God's maximum glory.

1. Had you ever realized before that God has called you to His work right now, right where you are? Or is this the first time you understood that truth?

_____

_____

_____

_____

_____

2. What was your response, individually and together?

_____

_____

_____

_____

_____

_____

3. Where did your discussion take you spiritually?

_____

_____

_____

_____

_____

YOUR MARRIAGE'S MISSION FIELD IS RIGHT WHERE YOU ARE, RIGHT NOW.

DAY 36

DEFINING DEVOTION

Three things will last forever—faith, hope, and love—and
the greatest of these is love.

1 Corinthians 13:13 NLT

Wow, I *love* the desserts at that restaurant."
"I just *love* their new line of clothing."
"I *love* his character in that movie. So awesome."
"I absolutely *love* it when we get to leave work early."
"I *love* you, too, honey."

There are so many words in the English language that
require varied versions for us to be able to effectively express
different levels of meaning. Today's informal and loose format
of communication, particularly influenced by texting and social
media, has only complicated our ability to converse.

The word *love* is most certainly very high up on that list of
words with multiple meanings. To someone just learning our
language, the person could be confused into thinking that a
husband or wife loves a chocolate cake on an equal level with

the person with whom he or she is living life. The various connotations of "love," connected to all sorts of insignificant material items and random strangers, can leave us questioning how truly intentional and sincere our "I love you's" actually are.

Oftentimes, in the very serious and candid conversations between parents and their adult children about becoming engaged to be married or a pastor talking with a church member contemplating marriage, the vital and final question is, "I understand you love this person, but are you *in* love?"

So in reality, we have actually found a way in our culture to distinguish between having *a* love for someone and deciding when we have found *the* love of our life. We can likely let go of someone we just care deeply about, but losing "the one" is an entirely different matter when we are *in* love.

For Christians in a growing relationship with God, the understanding of authentic love is constantly deepening to reach further and further into our hearts as well as expanding ever wider to encompass the world we are called to reach. Sharing life with another believer in a marriage relationship makes this transformation have an even greater and more beautiful meaning.

Faith, hope, and love interweave in our lives, each building on the other. When we strengthen faith, we grow in hope and love. This statement is interchangeable with all three of these beautiful words.

Today's verse in *The Message* states, "Trust steadily in God, hope unswervingly, love extravagantly. And the best of the three is love." Thank God that you both can intimately know the Object of your faith and trust, the Focus of your hope, and the Author of your love. Thank Him also that you have been given these three as eternal gifts, directly to your heart from His.

Hold each other's hands, look straight into each other's eyes, and with all the sincerity in your soul, take turns saying, "I want you to know that I not only love you, but I am *in* love with you." You might be quite surprised at how different that phrase sounds and feels as it comes out of your mouths and then how most especially it is received. If authentically expressed, there is a strong likelihood that you will go to a new level in your relationship with one simple but profound sentence.

1. Why do we perceive a difference between saying, "I love you" and being *in* love?

_____

_____

_____

_____

_____

_____

_____

_____

_____

_____

2. How did saying, "I am in love with you" feel different from the usual "I love you"?

_____

_____

_____

_____

_____

_____

3. What are some ways you can express love to one another to bring new meaning to your words?

_____

_____

_____

_____

_____

LOVE THE LOVE
OF YOUR LIFE
EXTRAVAGANTLY.

DAY 37

NAVIGATING
THE NONVERBAL

If you have any encouragement from being united with Christ, if any comfort from his love, if any common sharing in the Spirit, if any tenderness and compassion, then make my joy complete by being like-minded, having the same love, being one in spirit and of one mind. Do nothing out of selfish ambition or vain conceit. Rather, in humility value others above yourselves, not looking to your own interests but each of you to the interests of the others. In your relationships with one another, have the same mindset as Christ Jesus.

Philippians 2:1–5

Attitudes are one of the most intriguing and interesting parts of the human personality. We can spot a great one or a crabby one from across the room. Words such as *whatever*, *sorry*, and *fine* can take on entirely different meanings based on the attitude of the one speaking—good or bad. Facial expressions, vocal inflections, body language, and countenance can all communicate attitude without a word being spoken. We know when we are having a bad attitude without anyone having to tell us, even though they might, much to our dismay. But when we are having a great attitude, everyone will know that as well. We learn early in life to read people in this way, so attitudes become obvious to us all and one of the strongest forms of nonverbal language we have.

In today's scripture, Paul's words to the church at Philippi included positive qualities such as encouragement, comfort, fellowship, tenderness, compassion, and humility. As he so often did, he went on to talk about the other side of the subject, avoiding such things as selfishness and pride. But Paul ended his exhortation by calling all believers to an *attitude*, specifically, the attitude of Christ.

We would all agree that God wants our actions to reflect the life and behavior of Christ. Those things that people see us do in the physical realm are important for our witness. But when we say that God wants our ongoing attitude to reflect the *mind* of Christ, how He *thinks*, that concept dives down much deeper into our souls and challenges what goes on in our thoughts. But even deeper, God's Spirit wants to saturate who we are to the point that He is involved in the very motives that drive all that we are, from attitudes to actions.

Apply today's passage to your marriage, as if Paul were speaking directly to both of you. Take a moment to evaluate and inventory your lives with his four "if" statements. Which of these areas are strong and growing? Where are you weak and struggling? And then the big questions for today: How would you describe the overall attitude of your marriage? Where would you land on a scale of 1 to 10? Close by affirming one another in the areas where either of your attitudes is positive and contagious.

1. Had you ever thought before about having the *attitude* of Christ? Why or why not?

_____

_____

_____

_____

_____

_____

_____

_____

_____

_____

2. Was there anything revealing to you in evaluating attitudes together?

_____

_____

_____

_____

_____

_____

3. How might evaluating your attitudes have a powerful effect on your actions?

_____

_____

_____

_____

_____

_____

ACTING LIKE JESUS BEGINS WITH THINKING LIKE JESUS.

A LONG LINE OF LOVE

"At last!" the man exclaimed. "This one is bone from my bone, and flesh from my flesh! She will be called 'woman,' because she was taken from 'man.'" This explains why a man leaves his father and mother and is joined to his wife, and the two are united into one. Now the man and his wife were both naked, but they felt no shame.

Genesis 2:23–25 NLT

Today, we sometimes hear people refer to marriage as an archaic, outdated, unnecessary institution. So especially in the Christian community, we must remind ourselves of the origin of the marital covenant. When a couple comes together at the altar "in the sight of God and these witnesses," the history of that ceremony goes all the way back to the very first couple, who were married in what was the most beautiful wedding venue ever in history.

In Genesis, the only time God viewed any of His creation and did not say "it is good" was when He saw that Adam was alone in his kind. God created all humankind in His image, but not His kind, in that God is spirit, while humanity is mind, body, and spirit.

So God formed all the animal kingdom and had Adam name them. But at the end of what must have been quite a long and grueling session of inventing new words, God saw none of these was right for Adam. Then God had a brilliant idea. He created woman! Adam's response when he saw her says it all: "At last!"

At a wedding, we don't have to hear the pianist change songs to know when the bride has appeared at the back of the room with her father. Why? Because facing toward the front, everyone sees the groom suddenly light up, his face beaming at the vision he has the privilege to see. For the soon-to-be husband, this exciting moment overwhelms him in a heartbeat when his eyes meet hers. She is beautifully adorned in her wedding dress, with every detail about her expressing perfection to him.

As the wedding guests stand to honor the bride's entrance, all eyes look away from him and are now fixed on her. She is proud, emotional, and radiant in her love as she locks eyes with her groom.

Those feelings and emotions, placed on full display at every wedding, are a beautiful duplication and reflection of that day in the garden when God, Adam, and Eve all agreed that now, this was indeed good.

When the days get mundane and life starts to take its toll on the closeness and intimacy in your marriage, today's "Creating Connection" is a great way to revive and restore one another.

Creating Connection

On a previous day, we encouraged you to look back at your wedding ceremony. Today is about talking through the personal emotions you felt toward each other on that day. Take some time to share what you felt the first time you saw each other and what went through your minds and hearts during the processional, vows, and exchange of rings. Reliving your emotions on your wedding day can be an amazing reminder of your love and all God has done in your lives in bringing you together to bless you as one.

1. Why do you suppose sharing memories together can have such a powerful impact on present feelings?

_____

_____

_____

_____

_____

_____

_____

_____

_____

2. How did sharing your past memories together affect you both?

_____

_____

_____

_____

_____

3. Are there any other connections you see between the passage in Genesis and your own wedding or relationship?

_____

_____

_____

_____

_____

GOD LOOKS AT YOUR MARRIAGE EVERY DAY AND SAYS, "IT IS GOOD."

DAY 39

OUR HOURS

Lord, remind me how brief my time on earth will be. Remind me that my days are numbered—how fleeting my life is. You have made my life no longer than the width of my hand. My entire lifetime is just a moment to you; at best, each of us is but a breath.

Psalm 39:4-5 NLT

As today's scripture says, our time on earth is short. It is the same for us all. We are on equal ground in the amount we have available: 24 hours in a day; 168 hours in a week; 8,760 hours per year. Time is a gift that cannot be stockpiled, depletes on its own, and, especially in this fast-paced era, never seems to be sufficient to accomplish all we have to do.

Time can be the source of a multitude of marital issues. In our relationships, the amount of time available for each other and the choice of how to spend it together can be an emotionally charged, ongoing struggle.

Some spouses value a quantity of time spent, while others are all about quality. Some are very independent and need a lot of "me time." Rarely do both mates in a marriage view the time spent together and apart exactly the same.

Here are three C's to help you navigate your marriage's test of time. These flow in order as well as interweave and overlap.

1. *Communicate*

   All too often when a sore spot, such as time commitments, start to challenge a relationship, one or both partners will opt to avoid conflict by not talking about the issue at hand. Marriage is just like international peace talks—progress is only being made when both parties are at the table. Talking and listening to each other's emotions, feelings, and facts are vital to finding peace.

2. *Compromise*

   Hearing each other out and being willing to give ground and sacrifice is what real love is all about. Ironically, both spouses *giving* ground to the other allows both to *gain* ground as well. One spouse constantly giving in to the other never results in a healthy relationship. Choose to meet in the middle as much as possible when you communicate about an important issue.

3. *Commitments*

   While you could likely use a fresh reminder of encouragement on the first two points, the third could be the most important of all. Discuss your commitments honestly and rationally. Remove emotion as much as possible. At the top of your list are two things: marriage and job. If you are parents, the children are placed in priority in between the two. You have to go to work to make money, and your marriage should supersede everything else, with your children being next. The application of this step is today's "Creating Connection."

At the top of your list, write two things: *marriage* and *job*. If you have children, write *parents* in between those two words. Next, both of you need to write down every activity in which you take part—together and individually—in the course of a normal week. In most marriages, time conflicts are found in individual choices. Together, agree on the activities that have to stay on the list. Now, individually prioritize the rest of your list. Decide what you are willing to give up or discuss letting go. Work through this process together, communicating and compromising until you both agree on your commitments—together and individually. Remember: investing time in your marriage will provide more no-regrets returns to you both than any other relationship or activity in which you could ever take part.

1. Was this exercise difficult for you? Why or why not?

_____

_____

_____

_____

_____

_____

2. What were the easiest and the hardest parts?

_____

_____

_____

_____

_____

_____

3. Did you arrive at an agreeable place in your priorities for time?

_____

_____

_____

_____

_____

_____

AS GO OUR HOURS, SO GO OUR LIVES.

THE DECIDING FACTOR

We can make our own plans, but the LORD gives the right answer. People may be pure in their own eyes, but the LORD examines their motives. Commit your actions to the LORD, and your plans will succeed.

Proverbs 16:1–3 NLT

Making decisions and evaluating choices create some of the constant stresses and issues we deal with in our marriages. And often, the sheer volume of decisions at hand is overwhelming. Will we take a decision too lightly, make it hastily without enough information, and then regret it for years? Or stress, worry, and lose sleep for a week, struggling over a crossroads? Point A or B? Success or failure? One of our toughest jobs is making the hard decisions together when so much can be riding on what we choose.

Here are four practical questions to help you navigate life decisions together.

1. *Has God already given you the answer?*

    The Bible has literally thousands of commands, precepts, and principles for how to live. Seeking out and searching in God's Word can bring many of our answers to light. While there certainly won't be a chapter and verse for "Lord, should we buy this house or not?" there is plenty of practical advice on *how* to best make a major decision. When faced with a tough choice, dig into the Word and ask God for His wisdom.

2. *Has God taught you anything in the past that could apply to your current decision?*

    God loves us enough to often work in patterns in our lives, so we can determine when He is at work versus when it's our own doing. Watch for those familiarities, and learn His ways in your life. He knows you, so He's constantly leaving you a trail to His path. Your past and God's presence can bring His light into your future.

3. *Has God already made provision for what you are asking?*

    This is applied when you are looking not just for an answer but actual provision for a need. There are many times in life where He has already provided, and we just haven't put two and two together yet. For example, a couple has a sudden financial need and begins to pray for provision, all the while forgetting that last month a surprise bonus was paid at work that they decided to earmark for vacation. Sometimes God provides His answers in advance of the need, and we can't overlook those connections.

4. *Why would God not want you to do it?*

    Looking at a decision from the other side can sometimes help you see the right choice. While it is fine to discuss why God might not want you to do something and evaluate the potential problems as well as blessings, there are times when He wants us to move forward in faith. We just need to give Him authority over our steps. Walking is simply a repeated pattern of the same movement.

As today's verses tell us, the Lord has the right answers for our lives, and we will find them when we commit our actions to Him.

Creating Connection

Discussing and praying together to make the right decision can be a spiritually bonding dynamic in marriage. Is there a decision on the table in your home right now? Use the four questions and explanations in the previous section to work through your decision. By working through these questions, open dialogue and honest prayer will not only help you make a mutual decision, but also grow you together in relationship and maturity in the Lord.

1. Did filtering your choices through the questions help? How?

_____

_____

_____

_____

_____

2. Which question helped the most?

_____

_____

_____

_____

_____

3. Do you as a couple need to become more consistent in prayer and searching God's Word for the answers you need in life? If so, discuss how.

_____

_____

_____

_____

_____

GOD'S WILL IS NOT HIDE-AND-SEEK BUT SEEK-AND-FIND.

DAY 41

A COUPLE'S CALLING

When Joseph and Mary had done everything required
by the Law of the Lord, they returned to Galilee to their
own town of Nazareth. And the child grew and became
strong; he was filled with wisdom, and the grace of God
was on him.

Luke 2:39–40

One of the greatest marriages in the Bible is often over-
shadowed for obvious reasons. When we focus solely on
the relationship of Joseph and Mary in the Gospels, we find
a deep and committed love for one another and for God. No
wonder the Father chose these two.

In those days, an engagement had the legality of a marriage,
but the couple lived apart until the wedding. When Mary said
to Joseph that an angel had told her she was pregnant with
the Messiah, imagine how that must have sounded to him. But
Mary's being quick to confide in Joseph, and tell her husband-
to-be the truth, no matter how bizarre it might sound, showed
her deep care, respect, and trust for him.

At first assuming some sort of infidelity, he was heart-broken to divorce Mary and legally end the betrothal. But Joseph put her needs first to try to minimize her disgrace. Then the angel visited Joseph in a dream to confirm Mary's news. Joseph immediately chose to obey God and wed Mary. Joseph even decided to abstain so there would be no question regarding her testimony as to the Source of the pregnancy, even though the angel never told him to take such action.

As the couple traveled to Bethlehem for the census (since Joseph was a descendant of King David), found the stable, experienced Jesus' birth, and witnessed the visit from the shepherds called by the angels, we consistently see again and again their great care for one another and their new Son. At the required age, they took Jesus to the temple for the religious ceremonies.

In Joseph and Mary's marriage, we see their strong communication, integrity, obedience, honor, and sacrificial love, always putting the other first. We must consider how strong their relationship must have been for God to choose them. If Jesus grew up healthy and strong, full of wisdom, with God's favor, as today's passage states, the marriage He witnessed in His raising would have been a major influence in His life.

Imagine for a moment your fiancée telling you that she is pregnant with God's child. Imagine your husband telling you that God spoke to him in a dream, and you have to pack up and flee the country for safety. When we read the Bible, we must never remove human emotions, logic, and reason from the stories of the quite normal people in them. This element of Scripture can encourage us in marriage to obey God, even when the assignment doesn't make sense to us.

Joseph and Mary's calling as a couple was clear—raise the Messiah as their own to adulthood under God's authority. What is God's calling in your marriage? What ministry burns in your heart when you think about it or get to take part? Has He drawn you together to pursue a mission? Or has He placed individual passions in your hearts to minister in different ways while supporting each other in prayer? Discussing your spiritual gifts, passions, and calling to ministry should become a regular and fluid conversation in your home. Ask these questions and talk through this topic. Serving Christ together can strengthen and bring His favor to your relationship in amazing ways. The God of Mary and Joseph is the God of your marriage too.

1. Have you ever discussed your spiritual passions and calling as a couple?

_____

_____

_____

_____

_____

_____

2. Are you in agreement about your mission, or is there some clarity that needs to come to either of you?

_____

_____

_____

_____

_____

3. What do you hope to see God do in your marriage through ministry together?

_____

_____

_____

_____

_____

GOD HAS CALLED YOU TO HIMSELF, ONE ANOTHER, AND HIS KINGDOM.

DAY 42

THE MARRIAGE MIRROR

"Why worry about a speck in your friend's eye when you have a log in your own? How can you think of saying, 'Friend, let me help you get rid of that speck in your eye,' when you can't see past the log in your own eye? Hypocrite! First get rid of the log in your own eye; then you will see well enough to deal with the speck in your friend's eye."

Luke 6:41–42 NLT

Who better to apply these verses to in our lives than the "friend" to whom we are married? And what relationship creates the "speck and log" scenario more than marriage?

God made marriage to be like a constant mirror for us, a reflection to see who we truly are, how we act in private, and to clearly see the best and worst of our lives for the purpose of growth and maturity.

How often do we begin to chafe over an action or a habit of our mate, allowing the annoyance and irritation to grow, only

165

to suddenly realize we do the very same thing? Those moments are often painful and humorous all at the same time. But just as Jesus so eloquently stated in His analogy, we easily zero in on the speck in our spouse's eye and not the log in our own, trying to avoid our own reflection in the mirror of marriage.

We must note that Jesus didn't just say that we become aware of the other person's issue; we take it a step further to point it out: "Friend, let me help you get rid of that speck in your eye." Funny how often our decision to volunteer help has more to do with the fact that we don't want to deal with the perceived problem any longer, far more than we want to help the other person improve his or her life. So, we begin to scope out something in our mate's life and make the heroic decision that we are going on a mission to change his or her "speck."

The problem with this intentional intrusion is that it never truly works in any relationship, but most especially inside the intimacy of marriage. Applying Jesus' teaching, our sole responsibility is to change our own lives with His help and healing. Our role in marriage is to pray for, support, encourage, show grace, and cheer on in an effort to submit every speck *and* log to the only One who can change our lives—Christ. Taking on the role of change-maker in another's life is taking charge of something we simply are not designed for or equipped to do.

Have you and your mate ever discussed your "rules of engagement" in communicating about the specks and logs in each other's lives? Have you created a forum for having tough talks? Allowing for honest and receptive discussions, so we don't become tempted to initiate pressure to change the other, will make for a happier and healthier relationship. Being proactive to form a plan about how to bring up potentially hurtful topics can actually help you avoid painful confrontations and damaging misunderstandings that can lead to far bigger problems. Likely both of you have different filters on how you receive difficult and sensitive words that can be construed as critical or cutting, so graciously talk this out to understand how best to communicate the tough topics.

1. What percentage of your arguments in the past have stemmed from the desire to change one another?

_____

_____

_____

_____

_____

_____

2. From this conversation, did you realize you each have a different way to receive difficult and personal discussions? What are these ways?

_____

_____

_____

_____

_____

_____

3. How do you think this new understanding of one another can benefit your marriage?

_____

_____

_____

_____

_____

TRADE IN YOUR MICROSCOPE FOR A TELESCOPE SO YOU CAN SEE GOD'S BIG PICTURE.

DAY 43

BEING STILL IN THE BATTLE

Moses answered the people, "Do not be afraid. Stand firm and you will see the deliverance the Lord will bring you today. The Egyptians you see today you will never see again. The Lord will fight for you; you need only to be still."

Exodus 14:13–14

The story of Moses and Pharaoh is legendary in historical and biblical contexts. As the final plague devastated Egypt, including Pharaoh's own household, the dictator relented and told Moses he could leave with his entire nation. The Israelites quickly packed their bags, plundered the Egyptians, and hit the road.

Finally granted their freedom, they began the first steps on their path to the promised land. But Pharaoh's defeat started to hurt his pride. Having second thoughts also about losing his slave labor force, he decided to recapture them. So, he set out with more than six hundred chariots and horsemen to head

Moses off. Meanwhile, the Israelites had arrived at the shores of the Red Sea and were camped out.

Imagine the shock and terror of hearing thousands of hoof-beats rumbling across the land, heading straight for them. With their lives suddenly threatened, the people decided that returning to slavery was better than dying on the seashore. But God gave Moses a plan even in this seemingly inescapable deathtrap, as we read in today's scripture.

Upon God's command, Moses stretched out his hand over the sea, and a strong wind not only pushed back the expansive waters to divide them in two, but also dried out the exposed ground. As the people stepped onto the seabed, the waters created dividing walls on each side. At some point, Pharaoh saw the opening and ordered his army to resume the chase.

As Moses reached the other side of the sea, while his people were walking out from the seabed, God told him to stretch out his hand once again. The Red Sea began to close back up—covering the Egyptian army that had already entered in force. God had once again created a path to life for His people when death seemed imminent from the enemy.

There are moments in all marriages when we are safe and secure, far away from any "Egypt" of the past and camped out by our own version of the Red Sea. But then suddenly, without warning, we are trapped between the encroaching enemy of a life crisis and what seems an impassable way out. When fear overwhelms us, we must remember that God will make a way where there seems to be no way. We need only to remember: *The LORD will fight for you; you need only to be still.* Our faith in Him, no matter how small, can connect with His provision and protection to help us get to the other side of whatever we are facing.

Recall some of the "Red Sea" moments in your life together. What did you do? What did you see God do? What did you learn? How did your faith change? Your relationship? Keeping a journal where you write down the victories and challenges you face together could encourage and inspire you in your relationship not only with one another but also with God. Write down what He does in each situation. Commemorate how He made a way for you in the most difficult times. Tell of His faithfulness to always see you through to the other side.

1. How did recalling your moments when God came through in a crisis encourage you?

   _____

   _____

   _____

   _____

   _____

   _____

   _____

   _____

2. How can your life journal help you when a new challenge arises?

_____

_____

_____

_____

_____

3. How can your life journal leave a spiritual trail for your family in the future?

_____

_____

_____

_____

_____

THE LORD WILL FIGHT FOR YOU. YOU NEED ONLY TO BE STILL.

DAY 44

PLANTING PATIENCE

Blessed is the one who trusts in the LORD, whose confidence is in him. They will be like a tree planted by the water that sends out its roots by the stream. It does not fear when heat comes; its leaves are always green. It has no worries in a year of drought and never fails to bear fruit.

Jeremiah 17:7–9

At the Royal Botanic Gardens at Kew in the United Kingdom, they have a plant called the Agave franzosinii. As a young specimen, it grew at a rate of three feet a week. After it reached the height of the roof of the greenhouse where it was located, the caretakers removed a panel to let the plant grow outside the structure. Eventually it slowed its rapid rate of growth, and the staff then waited for the day when the flowers would bloom at the very top. Finally, three-inch, yellow, trumpet-shaped flowers appeared. What's the big deal, you ask? The length of time between the plant's beginning and its blooms was forty years![5]

When we hear of marriages reaching the forty-year mark and above, we have great respect for those relationships because we all understand what it takes for two people to stick it out together for that long. U.S. Census Bureau information tells us that the average length of a marriage today that ends in divorce is eight years, and the median age for a first divorce is thirty.[6]

Aside from marriages that end due to abusive or immoral circumstances, the key questions that must be asked are: Is eight years long enough to establish a deep level of intimacy or to bloom? Are most people under the age of thirty today emotionally equipped and mature enough to see past immediate problems and look for long-term solutions? And the final question: is eight years giving up too soon before life has provided enough experiences to create a true bond?

By the time most young couples get to the altar, they are excited about the opportunity to live together and explore life as one. This motivation creates a rapid growth rate for a marriage early on. But as the new wears off, life settles in, and familiarity takes hold, this growth often slows down. The key to success is to keep feeding, nurturing, and caring for the relationship at the same pace you did when growth was easy and quick. If there is any relationship in society that needs, requires, and takes time and constant care, it is the intimacy of marriage.

We have to love our spouses enough to commit to patience and grace as we wait for our relationship to bloom! As today's scripture states, when we trust in the Lord and place our confidence in Him, we can be like a tree planted by the water that does not need to fear or worry and will continually bear fruit.

Together, talk about the "blooms" in your marriage—the big victories, the days when you pressed on and endured tough times, the memorable key moments when you both sensed your oneness and love for one another. Next, discuss the seasons of growth between the blooms. Connect the work and commitment you walked through to get you to the places of blooming. What resources nurture your relationship and sustain you? See how God uses all the seasons in life to help your relationship "never [fail] to bear fruit."

1. How did your growth seasons compare to your blooming moments in time span?

_____

_____

_____

_____

_____

_____

_____

_____

_____

2. What was your response to recalling the "blooms" in your marriage?

_____

_____

_____

_____

_____

_____

3. How could regularly talking through your collective growth encourage your future as a couple?

_____

_____

_____

_____

_____

_____

HOLD TIGHT TO ONE ANOTHER IN TOUGH TIMES, AND THE WORK WILL BE WORTH THE WAIT.

DAY 45

FULL AND OVERFLOWING

"Give to others, and God will give to you. Indeed, you
will receive a full measure, a generous helping, poured
into your hands—all that you can hold. The measure you
use for others is the one that God will use for you."

Luke 6:38 GNT

From Darren's journal:

*To my Heather: You are amazing. I can't even
begin to tell you how happy I am that you said yes to
me years ago. Now, I love you even more. I shudder to
think where I would be in life had you not come into it.
You are my best friend, and have been my rock during
this deployment. The way you've handled our family,
and the way you've handled me when I've gotten out
of line, have only made me love you more. Thank you
for your grace and elegance. I know a marriage is a
dance, a give and take. But I think you have given way*

more than I have. Becoming a single parent for 15 months is difficult enough, but you live every day with the crippling fear that someone from the Army may knock on your door with the worst news imaginable. You, not me, are the true hero of our family.

You are stunningly beautiful. I remember seeing you for the first time. You walked up and took my breath away. I was speechless. I knew I was in the presence of someone special. Please forgive me for the times I've taken you for granted and treated you less than what you deserve. I wish there were a better set of words to communicate "I Love You." If so, that's what I would say to you.

We are familiar with the old adage: "Absence makes the heart grow fonder." But when you consider the very real possibility of losing the one you love, another dimension is added to those emotions. Darren's distance had caused him to reflect on everything from his intense feelings the first time he met Heather all the way to his growing appreciation of who she had become since those early days of their relationship. What he thought was the absolute best for him got even better over time. That is what God, the Creator and Author of love, can do with and in a couple who give their hearts, lives, and marriage to Him.

Our society has become so what's-in-it-for-me that we can too often find ourselves wanting to invest 10 percent in a relationship while expecting a 100 percent return from the other person. In the healthiest and most successful marriages, we will most often find that this Luke 6:38 principle is being applied by both spouses, with each being more concerned about their own input to the relationship rather than focusing only on the other's output. That mind-set and state of the heart make for indivisible marriages. And we must always stay focused on the first word Jesus spoke in today's verse: *give*.

Creating Connection

Each of you write a short letter to the other, recalling the first time you met, how you felt, what you thought, and your feelings and emotions following that day. If you like, you can go ahead and move into what you currently love and appreciate about your mate, focusing on words of affirmation, just as Darren did for Heather. But the key point of today is to remember and recite those first moments when your heart's desire was to give "a full measure, a generous helping," "all that you [could] hold" to this new person you had just met.

1. How did recalling the memories make you feel?

_____

_____

_____

_____

_____

_____

2. How did writing these words help you appreciate your relationship today?

_____

_____

_____

_____

_____

3. What did you see in your mate's response to your letter?

_____

_____

_____

_____

_____

YOU CAN NEVER OUT-GIVE GOD, BUT IT CERTAINLY MAKES LIFE FUN TO TRY.

DAY 46

NO EXCUSES FOR YOUR NETS

As they went on their way, a man said to Jesus, "I will follow you wherever you go." Jesus said to him, "Foxes have holes, and birds have nests, but the Son of Man has no place to lie down and rest." He said to another man, "Follow me." But that man said, "Sir, first let me go back and bury my father." Jesus answered, "Let the dead bury their own dead. You go and proclaim the Kingdom of God." Someone else said, "I will follow you, sir; but first let me go and say good-bye to my family." Jesus said to him, "Anyone who starts to plow and then keeps looking back is of no use for the Kingdom of God."

Luke 9:57–62 GNT

We can't buy the house unless we first prove we can make the payments. We won't get the job without presenting the proper credentials for the work. Parents can't adopt the child until they have laid their lives open for examination.

Missionaries can't reach their people group until they have proven their motives for ministry.

Counting the costs is a crucial life principle. Understanding the level of commitment required before the promise made is necessary for success.

Today's scripture tells the story of people who made excuses not to follow Jesus.

While at first glance Christ's responses might appear to be insensitive and harsh, we must remember He reads minds and He knows hearts. In each case, the circumstances given were excuses made to avoid or delay obedience. These accounts of people putting Jesus off makes the disciples' response even more amazing. When Jesus told them to follow Him, both Matthew and Mark record that "at once they left their nets and went with him" (Matthew 4:20; Mark 1:18 GNT).

There are countless testimonies out there such as, "Yeah, at one time I really felt called to the mission field, but then I got married" or "I was planning on becoming a pastor until I got married." Marriage and ministry should support one another and accelerate the couple's mission together, not put an end to a calling.

Did either of you have spiritual goals before marriage that you let go of? Did one of you sense a calling from God to a ministry or a particular mission field? With a loving mate and a God who promises to provide all your needs, these dreams shouldn't be dismissed. In fact, He brought you together to make a stronger team for His purposes. Maybe now is your time together to pursue God as never before. Regardless of how many years have passed or what your current circumstances are, incredible blessings await a couple fully surrendered to Him. No excuses for you, like the folks in today's passage. Be an example, like His disciples. Leave your "nets," whatever those may be, and follow Him.

Share any past spiritual commitments or callings you may have once had, even if you have never voiced them before. This is the perfect time to share your spiritual goals. Share any visions or dreams you have had for what you would want to accomplish for the kingdom. Determine what "nets" you might need to drop. In this particular conversation, don't allow topics such as money and extended family to dampen your discussion. This particular moment is about faith and what God wants to do in and through you both together. To live large, you have to dream big!

1. What new information was shared that had never been spoken before?

_____

_____

_____

_____

_____

_____

_____

_____

2. How do your individual callings and dreams connect together?

_____

_____

_____

_____

_____

_____

3. How can you take a practical step together toward these places of obedience?

_____

_____

_____

_____

_____

_____

DON'T TRY TO REKINDLE OLD COALS; JUST BUILD A NEW FIRE TOGETHER.

DAY 47

PRAY AND STAY

"Ask and it will be given to you; seek and you will find; knock and the door will be opened to you. For everyone who asks receives; the one who seeks finds; and to the one who knocks, the door will be opened. Which of you, if your son asks for bread, will give him a stone? Or if he asks for a fish, will give him a snake? If you, then, though you are evil, know how to give good gifts to your children, how much more will your Father in heaven give good gifts to those who ask him!"

Matthew 7:7–11

Michael Smalley of the Smalley Institute created a poll for Christian marriages in which he asked one specific question about their prayer life: "How often do you pray together as a couple each week (not including meals)? The results were: 69 percent said they never pray outside of meals; 25 percent said they did once a week; and 6 percent responded that they prayed three or more times a week. While available statistics on the divorce rate among couples who pray together regularly are often disputed, no one argues that number is very low, reportedly as low as 1 percent.[7] That is where the saying originates, "The family that prays together stays together."

So if even among Christian couples, only six in one hundred pray regularly, what creates this obvious struggle and separation regarding going to God together?

Praying several times a week about intimate details of your life before God and your spouse can certainly be intimidating at first, which might provide some insight as to why so many marriages won't commit to this spiritual discipline. But here's the amazing upside: committing to this level of spiritual intimacy together would, without question, improve and strengthen any marriage.

God offers the optimum opportunity to every couple. While we all have varying physical and mental limitations, there are no limitations on your spiritual life! Your marriage has the same prospect of growing and maturing in Christ as anyone's on the planet. The only limits are the level of obedience. God's goal is to help you be one of those 6 percent who pray together regularly.

Jesus spoke of prayer often, and He continually taught us how to have the proper perspective of God as a loving Father, who desires to give us His very best. But He also made it clear that our part in the relationship is to be proactive in regularly coming to Him with what is on our hearts.

As a couple, have you been asking, seeking, and knocking together? If so, then keep growing by doing so. If not, today is your day. Have you been afraid you'll get "stones" and "snakes" from God? Decide to believe that He wants to give you "bread and fish." Just as He did when He fed the five thousand in Matthew 14, He wants to multiply His good gifts into your marriage.

Creating Connection

Talk about your prayer life together. If anything is hindering you from the commitment to pray regularly during the week, what are those obstacles? The goal is to create not a religious exercise but a relational experience between the three of you—one another and God. Choose a day or days, a time, and a place to pray together. Don't be concerned with what you say or how you sound. Simply share your hearts before the God who made you, brought you together, and longs to bless you with His good gifts.

1. What would stop you from becoming a couple who prays together?

_____

_____

_____

_____

_____

_____

_____

_____

_____

2. What might God do in your lives if you committed to this level of prayer together?

_____

_____

_____

_____

_____

_____

3. What does your marriage stand to gain from growing together spiritually?

_____

_____

_____

_____

_____

_____

PRAY AS THOUGH YOUR MARRIAGE DEPENDS ON IT.

DON'T CROSS THE RIVER TILL YOU REACH IT

"Who of you by worrying can add a single hour to your life? Since you cannot do this very little thing, why do you worry about the rest? . . . And do not set your heart on what you will eat or drink; do not worry about it. For the pagan world runs after all such things, and your Father knows that you need them. But seek his kingdom, and these things will be given to you as well."

Luke 12:25–26, 29–31

Worry and stress have become national pastimes in our fast-paced and self-absorbed culture. We spend a great deal of time and energy fretting over what happened yesterday, what might happen today, and what we hope won't happen tomorrow.

In his book *Recollections of a Busy Life*, Horace Greeley related a story that Abraham Lincoln told when Greeley asked him if civil war was on the horizon.

Many years ago, when I was a young lawyer, and Illinois was little settled, except on her southern border, I, with other lawyers, used to ride the circuit; journeying with the judge from county-seat to county-seat in quest of business. Once, after a long spell of pouring rain, which had flooded the whole country, transforming small creeks into rivers, we were often stopped by these swollen streams, which we with difficulty crossed. Still ahead of us was Fox River, larger than all the rest; and we could not help saying to each other, "If these streams give us so much trouble, how shall we get over Fox River?" Darkness fell before we had reached that stream; and we all stopped at a log tavern, had our horses put out, and resolved to pass the night. Here we were right glad to fall in with the Methodist Presiding Elder of the circuit, who rode it in all weather, knew all its ways, and could tell us all about Fox River. So we all gathered around him, and asked him if he knew about the crossing of Fox River. "O yes," he replied, "I know all about Fox River. I have crossed it often, and understand it well; but I have one fixed rule with regard to Fox River: I never cross it till I reach it."[8]

Charles Swindoll once said, "Worry is assuming responsibilities . . . that God never intended for you to handle."[9] Stressing over all the physical needs and wants of life, especially in the area of finances, is one of the major pressures on any marriage. While choosing not to worry about the details of life can be a tough challenge, as a Christian couple, you must realize that Jesus' words in today's passage are meant for your good and personal peace as you learn together to trust Him completely with every single component of life.

Together, make a list of your most pressing worries and stresses going on right now in your lives and marriage. Separate them into long-term and short-term, or ongoing and immediate concerns. With these issues, how many of them are you "in the river" right now versus worrying about them "before you have crossed"? For which ones are you assuming responsibility that God never intended for you to handle? Take a look again at verse 31. How can you take your eyes off the worries, "seek his kingdom," and let God give you "these things"? One by one, pray and hand each stress on your list over to God, and then leave them with Him.

1. Did it help or overwhelm you to write down your worries? Why?

_____

_____

_____

_____

_____

_____

_____

2. How many were *current* stresses versus *coming* stresses? What might this tell you?

_____

_____

_____

_____

_____

_____

3. How did you feel after giving your worries to God?

_____

_____

_____

_____

_____

CONVERT YOUR WORRIES TO WORDS AND PRAY.

DAY 49

SOUL FOOD BUFFET

The Holy Spirit produces this kind of fruit in our lives:
love, joy, peace, patience, kindness, goodness, faithfulness, gentleness, and self-control.

Galatians 5:22–23 NLT

Today, we hear the word *notes* used to describe the taste and smell of an organic substance. Notes are used to describe the flavors and fragrances of wines, coffees, chocolates, honeys, teas, and even soaps. For example, a soap label reads, "seaside citrus, jasmine water, with notes of amber musk," or a high-end coffee label has the words "tamarind, with notes of butterscotch and raspberry." Notice that on each label there is fruit.

In Galatians 5, Paul tells us that the Holy Spirit creates spiritual fruit in us over time, including love, joy, peace, patience, kindness, goodness, faithfulness, gentleness and self-control.

You will never see an apple or orange tree eating its own fruit. First, the tree produces its distinct fruit because that is what it does by virtue of its very identity; and second, the fruit is made not to sustain the tree, but for others to enjoy and be fed.

Certainly if we as Christians exhibit and exude the fruit of the Spirit, our lives will be blessed, but we must realize that God gives us the nine fruits listed primarily for others to enjoy and be blessed by it, to "eat" of it. He does not grow His fruit in us for people to admire our fruit-making ability, but simply to point back to Him as the Creator. You have likely said of someone, "I just really enjoy being around her. She is such a joy" or "I like spending time with him because he has such a peaceful demeanor." The real blessing of our fruit comes when others enjoy what He has created in us.

Just as the orange tree doesn't actually produce the fruit but just gets to give birth to it, we cannot possibly make our own spiritual fruit either; whether oranges and apples or joy and gentleness, God is the Creator.

What might be the "notes" that are listed on the label of your life? Your marriage? Your home? Does your life exhibit joy with a hint of goodness? Does your marriage exude love with a strong flair of faithfulness? Do people say after spending time in your home that they felt peaceful? Just as a wine or a coffee cannot choose and write its own notes, but only the one who drinks them can, we cannot correctly discern what others taste of our lives, marriages, or homes. Our role is to be obedient to Christ and remain in Him as a branch is connected to the vine, as Jesus stated in John 15. Jesus will then go about producing the amazing fruit only He can create, blessing us, our marriages, and those in our lives, while also bringing glory to Him.

Creating Connection

Read Galatians 5:22–23 again, and then each of you write down at least three of the nine fruits from Paul's list that you feel are the strongest in your mate. When you are both finished, share your answers and explain why you chose the ones you did. If you are seeing growth in one of the fruits that has been weak or in an area where struggle has been present, encourage and point out the progress you have seen. Focus this time on affirmation and the fruit of the Spirit you enjoy from each other's growth in Christ.

1. Were there any surprises in the fruit that you see in one another?

_____

_____

_____

_____

_____

_____

_____

_____

_____

2. How might you proactively encourage each other in any weaker fruit?

_____

_____

_____

_____

_____

3. What might you do to bring more of the fruit of the Spirit into your home?

_____

_____

_____

_____

_____

TASTE AND SEE THAT THE LORD IS GOOD.
(PSALM 34:8)

Living Out Lordship Together

A Jew named Apollos, a native of Alexandria, came to Ephesus. He was a learned man, with a thorough knowledge of the Scriptures. He had been instructed in the way of the Lord, and he spoke with great fervor and taught about Jesus accurately, though he knew only the baptism of John. He began to speak boldly in the synagogue. When Priscilla and Aquila heard him, they invited him to their home and explained to him the way of God more adequately.

Acts 18:24-26

In the book of Acts, we are introduced to a couple named Priscilla and Aquila. There are two intriguing facts about their inclusion in Scripture. First, very few couples are mentioned together in the Bible, so it is significant when they are; and second, in a male-dominated society, Priscilla's name is listed first the majority of the time. From their introduction in Acts 18, every reference mentions them together, never separately.

Aquila was a Jewish man who had to leave Italy upon the deportation of his people by Caesar in Rome. We must assume Priscilla likely was a Jew as well. Regardless, we quickly see that both are Christ-followers. When Paul left Corinth for Cenchreae, they went with him for the sole purpose of spreading the gospel, particularly to the Gentiles. The first time the couple heard Apollos preach, Priscilla and Aquila recognized his passion and ability, but as mature believers, saw that he needed a little help. They "invited him to their home and explained to him the way of God more adequately" (Acts 18:26).

With further mentions in the books of Romans, 1 Corinthians, and 2 Timothy, we clearly see that Priscilla and Aquila had fully committed their lives and marriage to furthering the gospel. The impact this couple had on the spread of the story of Christ places them in your own spiritual lineage. Without couples such as this, we might never have heard the gospel.

Today, God's grand purpose and plan for their marriage is quite clear to us. But what story is God writing about your relationship? Is there, could there be, a far greater purpose for your life together? What is the true big picture of why God blessed you with one another?

God is both the Creator and the Catalyst for the abundant life Jesus described for us. He gives a heavenly perspective to all who will listen and obey His will, His ways, and His Word.

One of the purposes of this devotional has been to inspire and challenge you to a deeper place in your marriage as well as a deeper walk with God. What if, after these fifty days, your lives and marriage were never the same again because you allowed God to do a work as you never have before—together—just like Priscilla and Aquila? That, my friends, is totally possible because of Christ being alive in your marriage.

Creating Connection

Pray together about what God might have in store for you in the days ahead as you continue on in the truths and principles you have learned these past fifty days. Here is a guide to help you, if needed.

Father God, I know You have a far greater plan for our lives than we could ever ask or imagine. If there is something You want to show us or speak to us about how we can follow You closer, please give us ears to hear and eyes to see. Give us strength and boldness to walk in greater faith as we walk with You. We don't want to miss out on what You have for us, so please help us to receive all You have planned for us together. Thank You for saving us. Let Your Spirit be alive in us and our marriage, so that we may truly live. In Jesus' name, amen.

1. What is the most significant truth with which you have connected over the past fifty days?

   _____

   _____

   _____

   _____

2. Has God spoken anything specific to you together during this time?

_____

_____

_____

_____

_____

3. What steps do you need to take together to follow God into your future?

_____

_____

_____

_____

_____

BE HISTORYMAKERS AND WORLD CHANGERS AS YOU FOLLOW JESUS TOGETHER.

CONGRATULATIONS ON
COMPLETING FIFTY DAYS!

Indivisible was written and published to help you to discover the help, hope, and healing that the power of God can bring into your lives and your marriage. The simple goal was for you as a couple to have a greater and deeper understanding of what life looks like when you commit to an intentional daily relationship with Jesus Christ together.

We want to encourage you to continue your new habit of spending time together with God daily—reading His Word, praying, listening, journaling, applying what you hear, and growing in your faith, then taking all that He gives you and reaching your world together for Christ.

While devotional books like this are great resources, we want to challenge you to get to the place where you sit down together with God's Word to read, talk through your spiritual lives, and pray together. The Bible is the greatest Book ever written for life and marriage from the Creator and Author of love. God has something new to say to you every day through His Spirit.

We echo Paul's prayer for your relationship as you press on toward an *Indivisible* marriage.

I pray that out of his glorious riches he may strengthen you with power through his Spirit in your inner being, so that Christ may dwell in your hearts through faith. And I pray that you, being rooted and established in love, may have power, together with all the Lord's holy people, to grasp how wide and long and high and deep is the love of Christ, and to know this love that surpasses knowledge—that you may be filled to the measure of all the fullness of God.

Now to him who is able to do immeasurably more than all we ask or imagine, according to his power that is at work within us, to him be glory in the church and in Christ Jesus throughout all generations, for ever and ever! Amen. (Ephesians 3:16–21)

Notes

1. "Learn More About Giant Sequoias," Sequoia Ministries International, accessed January 16, 2018, http://sequoia ministriesinternational.org/about-us/learn-more-about-giant -sequoias.
2. Royal Society of Chemistry, "Nitrogen," Periodic Table, accessed January 18, 2018, http://www.rsc.org/periodic-table/element/7 /nitrogen.
3. Alfa Chemistry, "What Are the Chemical Properties of Glycerine?," *Quora*, accessed January 18, 2018, https://www .quora.com/What-are-the-chemical-properties-of-glycerine.
4. *Encyclopedia Britannica*, s.v. "Alfred Nobel," accessed January 18, 2018, https://www.britannica.com/biography/Alfred-Nobel.
5. Jasper Copping, "A 40-Year-Wait for Plant to Flower—and Then It Dies," *The Telegraph*, March 18, 2012, http://www .telegraph.co.uk/gardening/9150500/A-40-year-wait-for-plant -to-flower-and-then-it-dies.html.
6. McKinley Irvin Family Law, "32 Shocking Divorce Statistics," *Family Law Blog*, October 30, 2012, https://www.mckinleyirvin .com/Family-Law-Blog/2012/October/32-Shocking-Divorce -Statistics.aspx.
7. Michael Smalley, "Do You Know the Divorce Rate of Couples Who Pray Together?", Smalley Institute, accessed January 25,

2018, http://www.smalley.cc/do-you-know-the-divorce-rate-of
-couples-who-pray-together/; no longer accessible.

8. Horace Greeley, *Recollections of a Busy Life* (Whitefish, MT: Kessinger, 2006), 405.

9. Charles R. Swindoll, *Wisdom for the Way: Wise Words for Busy People* (Nashville: J. Countryman, 2001), 127.